From Ze
Dash Diet Hero

200 Easy and Healthy Low-Salt Recipes for Beginners

Phyllis Fletcher

Copyright © 2023 By Phyllis Fletcher

All rights reserved
The content contained within this book may not be reproduced, duplicated or transmitted without direct written permission from the author or the publisher.
Under no circumstances will any blame or legal responsibility be held against the publisher, or author, for any damages, reparation, or monetary loss due to the information contained within this book. Either directly or indirectly. You are responsible for your own choices, actions, and results.

Legal Notice:
This book is copyright protected. This book is only for personal use. You cannot amend, distribute, sell, use, quote or paraphrase any part, or the content within this book, without the consent of the author or publisher.

Disclaimer Notice:
Please note the information contained within this document is for educational and entertainment purposes only. All effort has been executed to present accurate, up to date, and reliable, complete information. No warranties of any kind are declared or implied. Readers acknowledge that the author is not engaging in the rendering of legal, financial, medical or professional advice. The content within this book has been derived from various sources. Please consult a licensed professional before attempting any techniques outlined in this book.

By reading this document, the reader agrees that under no circumstances is the author responsible for any losses, direct or indirect, which are incurred as a result of the use of the information contained within this document, including, but not limited to, — errors, omissions, or inaccuracies.

Table of Contents

Introduction 7

Chapter 1: The Power of the DASH Diet in My Life 8

Chapter 2: The Science and Principles of the DASH Diet 10

Scientific Basis of the DASH Diet 10

Principles of the DASH Diet. 11

Intended Audience of the DASH Diet 12

Chapter 3: Getting Started with the DASH Diet 13

Common Questions Readers May Have Along the Way 15

Chapter 4: Foods Allowed and Prohibited on the DASH Diet 18

The Most Effective 21-Day Meal Plan 19

Breakfast Recipes 22
Avocado and Egg Toast 22
Aromatic Breakfast Granola 22
Fruits and Rice Pudding 23
Oatmeal Banana Pancakes .. 23
with Walnuts 23
Bagels Made Healthy 23
Blueberry Whole Wheat Waffles 24

Asparagus Omelet 25
Blueberry Muffins 25
Whole Wheat Baking Powder Biscuits 26
Bean Frittata 26
Buckwheat Crepes 27
Cereal with Cranberry Orange Twist 27
Whole Grain Pancakes 28
Mediterranean Toast 28
Raspberry Yogurt 28
Instant Banana Oatmeal 29
Dash Apple Pancakes 29
Scallions Omelet 30
French Toast with Applesauce 30
Carrot Cake Overnight Oats . 31
Egg Toasts 31
Smoked Salmon Egg Scramble with Chives and Dill 31
Peach Pancakes 32
Apple Oats 32
Banana & Cinnamon Oatmeal 33
Curry Tofu Scramble 33
Steel-Cut Oatmeal with Plums and Pear 33
Sweet Yogurt with Figs 34
Sweet Potatoes with Coconut Flakes 34
Southwest Tofu Scramble 35
Greek Yogurt Oat Pancakes .. 35
No-Cook Overnight Oats 36
Avocado Cup with Egg 36
Blueberry-Oatmeal Muffin in a Mug 37
Stuffed Breakfast Peppers 37

Breakfast Splits 38
Savory Yogurt Bowls 38
Coconut Crepes 38
Apple-Apricot Brown Rice
Breakfast Porridge 39
Quinoa Bowl 39

Appetizers, Snacks, and Sides 41
Turmeric Endives 41
Lemon Asparagus 41
Creamy Broccoli Cheddar Rice 41
Stuffed Sweet Potatoes 42
Chili Broccoli 43
No-Mayo Potato Salad 43
Parmesan Endives 44
Sweet Potatoes and Apples ... 44
Coconut, Strawberries, and Chocolate 45
Roasted Turnips 45
Balsamic Cabbage 46
Avocado, Tomato, and Olives Salad 46
Peanut and Chocolate Squares 47
Simple Pear Crumble 47
Spanish rice 48
Cilantro Lime Rice 49
Lime Carrots 49
Choco-Fudge Cookies 50
Very-Berry Mug Cake 50
Zesty Yogurt Pots 51
Spinach and Endives Salad .. 51
Butternut Squash Apple Salad 52
Italian Roast Mushrooms 52
Apple Blue Cheese Salad 53
Spiced Fruity Cookies 53
Roasted Brussels Sprouts 54

Garlic Potato Pan 55
Moist Chocolate Brownies 55
Arugula Salad 56
Creamy Cauliflower Mash 56
Zucchini Tomato Bake 56
Paprika Brussels sprouts 57

Lunch Recipes 58
Tofu & Green Bean Stir Fry .. 58
Salmon and Edamame Cakes 58
Easy Salmon Steaks 59
Cauliflower "Mac and Cheese" Casserole 59
Danish Style Duck with Cucumber and Carrots 60
Roasted Mushroom Risotto . 61
Lentil Avocado Tacos 61
Japanese Potato and Beef Croquettes 62
Avocado Sandwich with Lemon and Cilantro 63
Paella with Chicken, Leeks, and Tarragon 63
Balsamic Chicken and Vegetables 64
Flat Bread Pizza 65
Simple Veal Chops 65
Grilled Flank Steak with Lime Vinaigrette 66
Chicken Vegetable Soup 66
Sesame Breadsticks 67
Spicy Chili Salmon with Lemon 67
Chicken and Broccoli 68
New York Strip Steak with Mushroom Sauce 68
Zucchini Pad Thai 69
Peppery Beef Tenderloin 70
Red Beans and Rice 70

Pork and Roasted Tomato Mix 71
Curried Chicken wrap 72
Healthy Vegetable Fried Rice 72
Roasted Brussels Sprouts, Chicken, and Potatoes 73
Spinach and Beef Meatballs . 73
Beef Pot Roast 74
Spicy Cabbage Dish 74
Healthy Avocado Beef Patties 75
Simple Pork and Capers 75
Buffalo Chicken Lettuce Wraps 75
Baked Whole Wheat Macaroni and Beef Casserole 76
Veggie Sushi 76
Almond Butternut Chicken .. 77
Cobb Salad 78
Baked Eggs in Avocado 79
Mediterranean Shrimp Pasta with Artichokes and Spinach. 79
Artichoke Spinach Chicken .. 80
Aromatic Spaghetti 80
Open-Faced Garden Tuna Sandwich 81
Chipotle Lettuce Chicken 81
Easy Roasted Salmon 82

Desserts 83
Cardamom Donuts 83
Ginger Cookies 83
Coconut Pudding 84
Sweet Zucchini Pie 84
Kale Chips 85
Chili Nuts with Ginger 85
Avocado and Chocolate Pudding 86
Amazing Granola 86

Banana Cake 86
Matcha-Coconut Muffins 87
Apple Cupcakes 88
Lemony Chickpea Dip 88
Blueberry Almond Flour Muffins 88
Rhubarb Pie 89
Elegant Cranberry Muffins ... 90
Cocoa Mug Cake 90
Mint Bars 91
Protein Bars 91
Avocado Salsa 92
Nut Cookies 92
Delicious Fruit Mousse 93
Easy Lemon Cream 93
Vanilla Apple Mix 94
Pumpkin Bars 94
Baked Tortilla Chips with Chili 95
Peanut Butter and Chia Pudding 95
Blueberry Curd 96
Refreshing Watermelon Sorbet 96

Dinner Recipes 97
Chinese-Style Beef Stir-fry ... 97
Peppered Filet with Red wine sauce 97
Chicken Tortilla Soup 98
Spicy Enchilada Bake 99
Dill Chicken Salad 100
Cucumber and Seafood Bowl. 100
Spicy Baked Sweet Potatoes . 101
Spicy Tomato Shrimp 101
Nutty Riced Vegetables 102
Cream Dredged Corn Platter 102
White Bean Stew 103
Tasty Roasted Broccoli 103
Pear Quesadillas 104

Parmesan Crusted Pork 105
Cajun Chicken and Rice 105
Currant Pork Chops 106
Mac and Chokes 106
Chicken and Mushroom Stew 107
Ethiopian Cabbage Delight ... 108
Healthy Mediterranean Lamb Chops 108
Walnuts and Asparagus Delight 109
Dash Diet Stewed Chicken Enchiladas 109
Family Meatloaf 110
Tuna Sandwich 111
Elegant Pumpkin Chili Dish . 111
Mediterranean Grilled Leg of Lamb 112
Tasty Tortilla Bake 113
Chicken Salsa 113
Turkey Wrap 114
Tuscan White Beans with Shrimp, Spinach, and Feta ... 114
Sweet & Sour Pork Chops 115
Middle American Pork and Beans 116
Chickpea Cauliflower Tikka Masala 117
Chicken and Jasmine Rice ... 118
Healthy Pork Fajitas 119
Zucchini Beef Sauté with Coriander Greens 119
Beef Stir Fry 120
Chili-Lime Grilled Pineapple 120
Italian Stuffed Portobello Mushroom Burgers 121
Chicken and Vegetable Rice Pilaf 122
Lean Meatballs in Tomato Sauce 122

Smoothies 124
Carrot-Cake Smoothie 124
Coconut Spiced Apple Smoothie 124
Ginger Berry Smoothie 125
Flaxseed & Banana Smoothie 125
Peanut Butter and Banana Smoothie 125
Pumpkin Spice Smoothie 126
Peaches and Greens Smoothie 126
Peanut Butter Banana Smoothie 126
Strawberry Yogurt Smoothie 127
Orange and Peach Smoothie 127
Banana-Peanut Butter 'n Greens Smoothie 127
Coco Strawberry Smoothie ... 128
Fruity Tofu Smoothie 128
Orange Juice Smoothie 129
Cantaloupe Dash Smoothie .. 129
Creamy Blueberry Oat Smoothie 129

Conclusion 131

Measurement Conversion Chart 134

Introduction

Hi there! I'm Phyllis Fletcher, a registered nutritionist passionate about helping people improve their health through the power of nutrition. With years of experience advising clients on health issues like obesity, diabetes, heart disease, hypertension, and high blood pressure, I've seen the positive impact of a healthy diet on people's overall well-being firsthand.

Since childhood, I've been fond of cooking and living a healthy lifestyle, and I've made it my mission to combine these two elements in my life and work. I earned my Bachelor's and Master's degrees in nutrition from Texas Woman's University, and I keep up with all the latest research and evidence-based practices in nutrition.

Throughout my years of practice, I've had the privilege of helping many people transform their lives for the better. In my books, I always strive to strike the right balance between a healthy diet and tasty food because I believe eating well should be enjoyable and sustainable in the long run. Many clients have valued my highly effective diet programs and helped them achieve their health goals.

I currently reside in Fairfield, Connecticut, where I enjoy spending my free time with my loving husband and two wonderful children and practicing yoga to maintain my physical and mental well-being. My main desire is to help people on their way to a healthy and fulfilling life, and I am happy to share my knowledge and experience with you in this book.

So, if you are suffering from high blood pressure, are overweight, or want to live a healthier lifestyle, I am here to provide practical tips, science-based advice, and delicious recipes to help you make positive changes to your health. Let's start this journey together and take the first steps towards a healthy and happy life with the DASH diet!

CHAPTER 1
The Power of the DASH Diet in My Life

As a registered nutritionist, I've seen firsthand the remarkable benefits of the DASH (Dietary Approaches to Stop Hypertension) Diet in transforming the health and lives of my clients. But it's not just something I preach to others; it's a way of eating that I've personally incorporated into my own life with remarkable results.

The DASH diet is not just another diet or a short-term way to improve your health. It's a scientifically proven approach to eating that focuses on whole, nutrient-rich foods and has been shown to effectively lower blood pressure, reduce the risk of heart disease, and improve overall health. And the best part? It's not about deprivation or strict rules, but rather about making sustainable, enjoyable changes to your eating habits.

I've personally experienced the power of the DASH Diet in my life. As someone with a family history of hypertension, I knew taking control of my diet was crucial for my long-term health. By using the principles of the DASH diet, I have significantly improved my blood pressure and overall health.

One of the key aspects of the DASH Diet is its emphasis on whole, minimally processed foods. I've prioritized filling my plate with an abundance of fruits and vegetables, whole grains, lean proteins, and healthy fats. I've found creative ways to incorporate these foods into my meals, from whipping up colorful and nutrient-packed salads to experimenting with new recipes with wholesome ingredients.

The DASH diet also involves reducing sodium, sugar, and unhealthy fats, which is very important when following this diet. I started to read food labels more carefully, reduced my consumption of packaged and processed foods, and became more careful about the amount of salt and sugar I added to my food. I've discovered delicious and satisfying ways to flavor my meals with herbs, spices, and other natural seasonings, without relying on excessive salt or sugar.

The DASH Diet has also encouraged me to be more mindful of portion sizes and eat mindfully. I've learned to listen to my body's hunger and fullness cues, and I try to eat slowly and savor each bite. This has helped me develop a healthier relationship with food, and I no longer feel the need to overeat or indulge in mindless snacking.

Aside from the physical health benefits, the DASH Diet has also positively impacted my mental and emotional well-being. Eating a balanced and nutritious diet has helped me maintain stable energy levels, improve my mood and enhance my overall well-being. I've also experienced the joy of trying new foods, discovering new flavors, and expanding my culinary horizons through the diverse array of foods encouraged in the DASH Diet.

In summary, the DASH diet has changed my life, personally and professionally. Its evidence-based principles have not only helped me manage my blood pressure and reduce my risk of heart disease but have also empowered me to make positive, sustainable changes to my eating habits. It's a way of eating that I wholeheartedly endorse and integrate into my daily life, and I'm excited to share the benefits of the DASH Diet with you in this book. Whether your goal is to improve your cardiovascular health, manage your weight, or live a healthier lifestyle, the DASH diet can be a powerful tool to help you achieve your health goals. In the following chapters, we'll delve deeper into the science, principles, and practical tips of the DASH Diet. I'll share my expertise, personal experiences, and delicious recipes to help you incorporate this approach into your life.

CHAPTER 2
The Science and Principles of the DASH Diet

As a registered nutritionist, my primary goal is to help people improve their health by sharing science-based information and guidelines on the DASH diet. This eating plan has been widely recognized for its effectiveness in reducing the risk of heart disease, lowering blood pressure, and improving overall health. Let's look at the unique features of the DASH diet and find out why it has become the gold standard for healthy eating.

Scientific Basis of the DASH Diet

The DASH diet is rooted in robust research conducted by the National Heart, Lung, and Blood Institute (NHLBI), which aimed to explore the correlation between diet and blood pressure. In the 1990s, the landmark DASH study conducted rigorous clinical trials that demonstrated the powerful impact of specific dietary patterns on reducing blood pressure. According to the study, a diet consisting of abundant vegetables, fruits, whole grains, lean proteins, and low-fat dairy products while limiting sodium, added sugars, and unhealthy fats can significantly lower blood pressure.

The principles of the DASH Diet are also supported by a large body of scientific evidence from various studies and research conducted worldwide. These studies have consistently shown that following the DASH Diet can improve blood pressure and other markers of heart health, such as cholesterol levels, insulin sensitivity, and overall cardiovascular risk.

Principles of the DASH Diet

The DASH Diet is a versatile and well-balanced eating regimen that prioritizes whole, minimally processed foods while restricting the intake of sodium, added sugars, and unhealthy fats. Its fundamental principles encompass:

Abundant Fruits and Vegetables: The DASH Diet encourages a generous intake of fruits and vegetables, which are rich in essential nutrients, fiber, and antioxidants. These plant-based foods are the foundation of the diet and should be consumed in various forms, including fresh, frozen, or canned, without added sugars or sodium.

Whole Grains: The DASH diet places a strong emphasis on the consumption of whole grains, which include brown rice, whole wheat, quinoa, oats, and barley. These grains are an excellent source of fiber, vitamins, minerals, and other beneficial compounds that support heart health and enhance overall well-being.

Lean Proteins: The DASH Diet recommends lean protein sources, such as poultry, fish, beans, lentils, nuts, and seeds. These protein-rich foods provide essential amino acids, healthy fats, and other nutrients without the added saturated fat and cholesterol found in fatty cuts of meat.

Low-Fat Dairy Products: The DASH Diet encourages the consumption of low-fat or fat-free dairy products, such as milk, yogurt, and cheese. These dairy products are rich in calcium, protein, and other essential nutrients while being lower in saturated fat compared to full-fat dairy options.

Limited Sodium: The DASH Diet promotes reducing the intake of sodium, a mineral that can contribute to high blood pressure. This involves minimizing the use of salt in cooking and opting for low-sodium or no-added-salt versions of foods, as well as being mindful of hidden sources of sodium in processed and packaged foods.

Limited Added Sugars and Unhealthy Fats: As per the recommendations of the DASH Diet, it is advised to restrict the consumption of added sugars, as well as unhealthy fats such as trans fats and saturated fats.

This involves reducing the consumption of sugary beverages, sweets, pastries, fried foods, and processed snacks, and opting for healthier fats, such as those found in avocados, nuts, and seeds.

Intended Audience of the DASH Diet

The DASH Diet is intended for anyone looking to improve their cardiovascular health, manage their blood pressure, or adopt a healthy eating pattern. It's a flexible and sustainable eating plan that people of all ages and backgrounds can follow. It is particularly beneficial for individuals with hypertension or at risk of developing high blood pressure and those with other risk factors for heart disease, such as obesity, diabetes, and high cholesterol.

The DASH Diet is also suitable for individuals looking to improve their overall health and well-being, regardless of their current health status. It can be customized to accommodate different dietary preferences, cultural backgrounds, and lifestyles, making it a versatile and inclusive eating plan.

In conclusion, the DASH Diet is scientifically proven and effective in promoting heart health and managing blood pressure. Its principles are based on extensive research and evidence, and it emphasizes the consumption of whole, nutrient-dense foods while limiting sodium, added sugars, and unhealthy fats. The DASH Diet is suitable for a wide range of individuals and can be tailored to fit various dietary preferences and lifestyles. By adopting the principles of the DASH Diet, you can take a proactive step towards improving your health and well-being, and I'm thrilled to guide you on this journey in the following chapters of this book.

CHAPTER 3
Getting Started with the DASH Diet

As someone who has been practicing and promoting the DASH Diet for many years, I understand that starting a new eating plan can sometimes feel overwhelming. However, incorporating the DASH Diet into your everyday life can be rewarding and beneficial. Let me share with you some practical advice based on my personal experience and common questions from readers like you on how to get started with the DASH Diet.

Educate Yourself about the DASH Diet

Before embarking on any new eating plan, it's essential to understand the principles, scientific basis, and guidelines of the DASH Diet. Familiarize yourself with the recommended food groups, portion sizes, and nutrient goals. Equipped with this knowledge, you will be empowered to make well-informed food choices and devise a balanced meal plan.

Assess Your Current Dietary Habits and Health Goals

Pause for a moment to contemplate your current eating habits and health aspirations. What are your strengths and areas for improvement? What motivates you to follow the DASH Diet? Setting realistic expectations and aligning your health goals with the DASH Diet will help you stay focused and committed.

Plan and Prepare Meals in Advance

Planning and preparing meals in advance can help you stay on track with the DASH Diet. Formulate a weekly meal plan, compile a grocery list, and ensure your pantry is stocked with DASH-friendly foods like fruits, vegetables, whole grains, lean proteins, and dairy products. Preparing meals at home affords you greater control over the ingredients and portion sizes and can be an enjoyable and imaginative means to experiment with new recipes.

Be Mindful of Sodium Intake

Sodium is a critical component of the DASH Diet, and it's essential to be mindful of your sodium intake. Exercise caution and thoroughly read food labels, opting for low-sodium or no-added-salt alternatives whenever feasible. Limit processed foods, fast foods, and salty snacks. Instead, season your meals with herbs, spices, and other flavor-enhancing techniques that are low in sodium.

Make Gradual Changes

Incorporating the DASH Diet into your lifestyle doesn't have to happen overnight. It's okay to start with small, achievable changes and gradually progress towards a more DASH-friendly eating pattern. For example, you can start by adding an extra serving of vegetables to your meals, switching to whole grains, or reducing your intake of sugary beverages. Consistency is key, and small changes can add up over time.

Stay Hydrated

Proper hydration is crucial for overall well-being and is an essential component of the DASH Diet. It is recommended to consume an adequate amount of water throughout the day to ensure optimal hydration. Sugary beverages, soda, and alcohol should be limited as they add unnecessary calories and sugar to your diet.

Listen to Your Body

Be mindful of your hunger and fullness cues, and practice mindful eating to foster a healthy relationship with food. Adopt a leisurely pace while eating, relishing each bite, and stop when you feel comfortably full, paying attention to your body's cues. Avoid eating when you're distracted, stressed, or emotional, as this can lead to overeating or mindless eating.

Seek Support and Guidance

It's always helpful to have support along the way. Consider partnering with a registered dietitian or healthcare provider who can provide personalized guidance, answer your questions, and help you stay accountable to your DASH Diet goals. Connect with other individuals who are following the DASH Diet for support and motivation.

Stay Positive and Be Kind to Yourself

It's important to remember that adopting a new eating plan requires time and effort. Be patient and kind to yourself, and celebrate even the smallest progress along the way. Don't beat yourself up for occasional slip-ups or setbacks. Stay positive, and focus on the long-term benefits of the DASH Diet for your health and well-being.

Common Questions Readers May Have Along the Way

Q: Can I still enjoy my favorite foods on the DASH Diet?

A: Yes, you can still enjoy your favorite foods on the DASH Diet! The DASH Diet is not about strict restrictions or deprivation. It's about making smart food choices and creating a balanced eating pattern. You can still incorporate your favorite foods in moderation while following the principles of the DASH Diet. Just be mindful of portion sizes and frequency of indulgence.

Q: Can I eat out while on the DASH Diet?

A: Yes, you can eat out while on the DASH Diet! Dining out can be challenging due to the high levels of sodium, unhealthy fats, and added sugars often present in restaurant meals. However, there are ways to make healthier choices. Look for restaurants that offer DASH-friendly options such as grilled or roasted lean meats, steamed vegetables, whole grain options, and salads with dressing on the side. Ask for modifications or substitutions to reduce sodium and unhealthy fats, and be mindful of portion sizes.

Q: Is the DASH Diet suitable for vegetarians or vegans?

A: Yes, the DASH Diet can be adapted for vegetarians or vegans! The DASH Diet emphasizes the consumption of fruits, vegetables, whole grains, nuts, seeds, legumes, and low-fat dairy products, making it easily adaptable to vegetarian or vegan eating patterns. Indeed, plant-based sources of protein, such as beans, lentils, tofu, tempeh, and quinoa, can serve as excellent substitutes for animal-based proteins in the DASH Diet. Just be sure to pay attention to nutrient balance and get enough protein, iron, calcium, vitamin B12, and omega-3 fatty acids from plant-based sources.

Q: Can I still enjoy alcohol on the DASH Diet?

A: The DASH diet suggests moderate alcohol consumption, but it's crucial to note that excessive intake of alcohol can lead to weight gain and other health problems. Hence, it is advisable to limit alcohol intake and opt for healthier alternatives like red wine, which has antioxidants. Remember, alcohol is high in calories, so it's important to consume it in moderation.

Q: Can I follow the DASH Diet if I have dietary restrictions or allergies?

A: Certainly, the DASH Diet can be customized to suit individual dietary restrictions or allergies. However, it's important to consult a registered dietitian or healthcare provider to create a personalized meal plan that meets your specific needs. With a little planning and the use of alternative options, such as different food groups, you can still adhere to the principles of the DASH Diet while following your dietary restrictions or allergies.

In conclusion, starting the DASH Diet can be a positive step towards improving your health and well-being. Educate yourself about the DASH Diet, assess your current habits and health goals, plan and prepare meals in advance, be mindful of sodium intake, make gradual changes, stay hydrated, listen to your body, seek support and guidance, stay positive, and be kind to yourself. With consistent effort, you can successfully incorporate the DASH Diet into your everyday life and reap the benefits of a healthy eating pattern. Remember, progress, not perfection, is the key. Best of luck on your DASH Diet journey!

CHAPTER 4
Foods Allowed and Prohibited on the DASH Diet

Allowed Foods:

1. Fruits: Apples, bananas, oranges, berries, grapes, melons, etc.

2. Vegetables: Leafy greens, broccoli, carrots, sweet potatoes, bell peppers, tomatoes, etc.

3. Whole Grains: Brown rice, quinoa, oats, whole wheat bread, whole grain pasta, etc.

4. Lean Proteins: Chicken breast, turkey, fish, beans, lentils, tofu, tempeh, etc.

5. Low-fat Dairy Products: Skim milk, low-fat yogurt, low-fat cheese, cottage cheese, etc.

6. Nuts and Seeds: Almonds, walnuts, chia seeds, flaxseeds, etc.

7. Healthy Fats: Avocado, olive oil, canola oil, etc.

8. Herbs and Spices: Basil, cilantro, parsley, rosemary, thyme, etc.

9. Limited Added Sugars: Occasionally using natural sweeteners like honey or maple syrup in moderation as per the DASH Diet guidelines.

Prohibited Foods:

1. High-Sodium Foods: Processed foods, canned soups, salty snacks, fast food, etc.

2. High-Fat Foods: Fried foods, high-fat dairy products, fatty cuts of meat, etc.
3. Added Sugars: Soda, candy, desserts, sugary beverages, etc.
4. Excess Alcohol: Heavy consumption of alcoholic beverages.
5. Processed Meats: Bacon, sausage, hot dogs, etc.

Foods High in Saturated Fats: Butter, coconut oil, palm oil, etc.

The Most Effective 21-Day Meal Plan

DAY	BREAKFAST	LUNCH	DINNER	SNACK
1	Avocado and Egg Toast	Tofu & Green Bean Stir Fry	Chinese-Style Beef Stir-fry	Carrot-Cake Smoothie
2	Aromatic Breakfast Granola	Salmon and Edamame Cakes	Peppered Filet with Red wine sauce	Turmeric Endives
3	Fruits and Rice Pudding	Easy Salmon Steaks	Chicken Tortilla Soup	Lemon Asparagus
4	Oatmeal Banana Pancakes with Walnuts	Cauliflower "Mac and Cheese" Casserole	Spicy Enchilada Bake	Ginger Cookies
5	Bagels Made Healthy	Danish Style Duck with Cucumber and Carrots	Dill Chicken Salad	Stuffed Sweet Potatoes
6	Blueberry Whole Wheat Waffles	Roasted Mushroom Risotto	Cucumber and Seafood Bowl	Chili Broccoli
7	Asparagus Omelet	Lentil Avocado Tacos	Spicy Baked Sweet Potatoes	No-Mayo Potato Salad

8	Blueberry Muffins	Japanese Potato and Beef Croquettes	Spicy Tomato Shrimp	Parmesan Endives
9	Whole Wheat Baking Powder Biscuits	Avocado Sandwich with Lemon and Cilantro	Nutty Riced Vegetables	Sweet Potatoes and Apples
10	Bean Frittata	Paella with Chicken, Leeks, and Tarragon	Cream Dredged Corn Platter	Coconut, Strawberries, and Chocolate
11	Buckwheat Crepes	Balsamic Chicken and Vegetables	White Bean Stew	Roasted Turnips
12	Cereal with Cranberry-Orange Twist	Flat Bread Pizza	Tasty Roasted Broccoli	Avocado, Tomato, and Olives Salad
13	Whole Grain Pancakes	Simple Veal Chops	Pear Quesadillas	Peanut and Chocolate Squares
14	Mediterranean Toast	Grilled Flank Steak with Lime Vinaigrette	Parmesan Crusted Pork	Simple Pear Crumble
15	Raspberry Yogurt	Chicken Vegetable Soup	Cajun Chicken and Rice	Spanish Rice
16	Instant Banana Oatmeal	Sesame Breadsticks	Mac and Chokes	Lime Carrots
17	Dash Apple Pancakes	Spicy Chili Salmon with Lemon	Chicken and Mushroom Stew	Choco-Fudge Cookies

18	Scallions Omelet	New York Strip Steak with Mushroom Sauce	Ethiopian Cabbage Delight	Very-Berry Mug Cake
19	French Toast with Applesauce	Zucchini Pad Thai	Healthy Mediterranean Lamb Chops	Zesty Yogurt Pots
20	Carrot Cake Overnight Oats	Peppery Beef Tenderloin	Walnuts and Asparagus Delight	Spinach and Endives Salad
21	Egg Toasts	Red Beans and Rice	Dash Diet Stewed Chicken Enchiladas	Paprika Brussels sprouts

Breakfast Recipes

Avocado and Egg Toast

Prep time: 5 minutes

Cook time: 5 minutes

Servings: 1

Ingredients:
- 2 eggs
- 2 slices of whole-grain bread
- 1 small avocado
- 1 tsp. freshly squeezed lime juice
- Black pepper, freshly ground

Directions:
1. Toast bread.
2. Cook eggs to personal preference, using a non-stick cooking spray instead of butter or oil, for 5 minutes.
3. Peel and mash avocado with pepper and lime juice.
4. Evenly spread the mashed avocado on both sides of each slice of toast.
5. Top each slice with a cooked egg.
6. Serve immediately.
7. Drizzle honey on top and enjoy.

Nutritional Info Per Serving:

Calories: 425, Fats: 22 g, Carbs: 41 g, Proteins: 21 g, Potassium: 1057 mg, Sodium: 301 mg

Aromatic Breakfast Granola

Prep time: 10 minutes

Cook time: 20 minutes

Servings: 2

Ingredients:
- 2 tbsp. avocado oil
- 1 tbsp. liquid honey
- 1/4 tsp. ground cinnamon
- 1/4 cup almonds, chopped
- 1 tbsp. chia seeds
- 1 tsp. sesame seeds
- 2 tbsp. steel-cut oats
- Cooking spray

Directions:
1. Heat up liquid honey and avocado oil to get a homogenous mixture.
2. Add almonds, sesame seeds, ground cinnamon, steel-cut oats, and chia seeds.
3. Stir until homogenous.
4. Spray the cooking spray on the baking tray and place the almond mixture inside.
5. Flatten it into a square shape.
6. Bake the granola for 20 minutes at 345°F.
7. Cut into servings.

Nutritional Info Per Serving:

Calories: 203, Fats: 11.4 g, Carbs: 22.3 g, Proteins: 5.7 g, Potassium: 93 mg, Sodium: 3 mg

Fruits and Rice Pudding

Prep time: 10 minutes

Cook time: 10 minutes

Servings: 3

Ingredients:
- ½ cup long-grain rice
- 1 ½ cup low-fat milk
- 1 tsp. vanilla extract
- 2 oz. apricots, chopped

Directions:
1. Pour milk and add rice to the saucepan.
2. Cover and cook the rice on medium-high heat for 10 minutes.
3. Add vanilla extract and stir.
4. Transfer the pudding to the bowls and top with apricots.

Nutritional Info Per Serving:
Calories: 171, Fats: 0.3 g,
Carbs: 32.9 g, Proteins: 6.4 g
Potassium: 452mg, Sodium: 156mg

Oatmeal Banana Pancakes with Walnuts

Prep time: 15 minutes

Cook time: 5 minutes

Servings: 8

Ingredients:
- 1 firm banana, finely diced
- 1 cup whole wheat pancake mix
- 1/8 cup walnuts, chopped
- ¼ cup old-fashioned oats
- Cooking spray
- ¼ cup pancake mix

Directions:
1. Prepare pancake mix as per the directions on the package, using whole wheat pancake mix.
2. Add oats, walnuts, and chopped bananas to the pancake mix.
3. Spray cooking spray on a griddle. When the griddle is hot, add ¼ cup of the pancake batter.
4. Cook until bubbles form on top and then flip the pancake. Cook for 5 minutes or until golden brown.
5. Serve right away

Nutritional Info Per Serving:
Calories: 260, Fats: 8 g
Carbs: 43 g, Proteins: 5 g
Potassium: 240mg, Sodium: 240mg

Bagels Made Healthy

Prep time: 5 minutes

Cook time: 26 minutes

Servings: 8

Ingredients:
- 1 1/2 cups warm water
- 1 1/4 cups whole wheat flour
- 2 tbsp. honey
- 2 cups whole wheat flour
- 2 tsp. yeast
- 1 1/2 tbsp. olive oil
- 1 tbsp. vinegar

Directions:
1. In a mixing bowl, mix warm water, wheat flour, honey, yeast, olive oil, and vinegar until well combined, forming a smooth dough.
2. Form balls from the dough and flatten them to form a bagel shape.
3. Make a hole in the middle of each bagel with your thumb, forming a donut shape.
4. After shaping the bagels, place them on a greased baking sheet and cover with a towel. Allow them to rise for 30 minutes.
5. Preheat your oven to 350°F.
6. Boil water in a large saucepan and place the bagels in it. Cook them for 1 minute on each side.
7. Finally, place the bagels on a baking sheet and bake them in the oven for 20 minutes.
8. Allow the bagels to cool before serving.

Nutritional Info Per Serving:
Calories: 220, Fats: 3 g
Carbs: 44 g, Proteins: 7 g
Potassium: 147mg, Sodium: 140 mg

Blueberry Whole Wheat Waffles

Prep time: 5 minutes
Cook time: 15 minutes
Servings: 8

Ingredients:
- 2 cups whole wheat flour
- 1 tbsp baking powder
- 1 tsp ground cinnamon
- 2 tbsp sugar
- 2 large eggs
- 3 tbsp unsalted butter, melted
- 3 tbsp nonfat plain Greek yogurt
- 1 1/2 cups 1% milk
- 2 tsp vanilla extract
- 4 oz blueberries
- Nonstick cooking spray
- 1/2 cup almond butter (maple flavored or unsweetened)

Directions:
1. Preheat your waffle iron.
2. Mix the wheat flour, sugar, baking powder, and ground cinnamon in a large bowl.
3. Mix the melted butter, milk, beaten eggs, Greek yogurt, and vanilla extract separately.
4. Mix the wet and dry ingredients until a dough forms, and add the blueberries.
5. Pour 1/3 cup of the batter onto the waffle iron, pre-coating it with non-stick

spray, and cook until the waffles are crispy and lightly browned.
6. Serve the waffles with 1 tbsp of almond butter on top.

Nutritional Info Per Serving:
Calories: 320, Fats: 12 g
Carbs: 43 g, Proteins: 10 g
Potassium: 335mg, Sodium: 210 mg

Asparagus Omelet

Prep time: 5 minutes

Cook time: 7 minutes

Servings: 3

Ingredients:
- 3 oz. asparagus, boiled, chopped
- ¼ tsp. ground paprika
- ½ tsp. ground cumin
- 3 eggs, beaten
- 2 tbsp. low-fat milk
- 1 tsp. avocado oil

Directions:
1. Heat up avocado oil in the skillet.
2. In the meantime, mix up eggs, ground cumin, milk, and ground paprika.
3. Pour the liquid into the hot skillet and cook for 2 minutes.
4. Add asparagus and cover.
5. Cook on low heat for 5 minutes and serve.

Nutritional Info Per Serving:
Calories: 160, Fats: 8 g
Carbs: 9 g, Proteins: 12 g
Potassium: 420mg, Sodium: 160mg

Blueberry Muffins

Prep time: 10 minutes

Cook time: 25 minutes

Servings: 12

Ingredients:
- 2 ripe bananas, mashed
- 1 cup unsweetened almond milk
- 1 tsp. vanilla extract
- ¼ cup pure maple syrup
- 1 tsp. apple cider vinegar
- ¼ cup unsweetened applesauce
- 2 cups almond flour
- 2 tbsp. coconut sugar
- 2 tsp. cinnamon powder
- 2 tsp. baking powder
- 2 cups fresh or frozen blueberries
- ½ tsp. baking soda
- ½ cup chopped walnuts (optional)

Directions:
1. In a bowl, combine the mashed bananas, almond milk, vanilla extract, maple syrup, apple cider vinegar, and unsweetened applesauce. Mix well.
2. Add almond flour, coconut sugar, cinnamon powder, baking powder, baking soda, and mix until just combined.

3. Gently fold in the blueberries and chopped walnuts (if using).
4. Divide the batter into muffin cups lined with paper liners.
5. Bake at 350 degrees F for 25 minutes, or until a toothpick inserted into the center comes out clean.
6. Allow muffins to cool before serving.

Nutritional Info Per Serving:
Calories: 160, Fats: 6 g
Carbs: 23 g, Proteins: 4 g
Potassium: 178 mg, Sodium: 110 mg

Whole Wheat Baking Powder Biscuits

Prep time: 5 minutes

Cook time: 10 minutes

Servings: 5

Ingredients:
- 1 egg white
- 1 cup white whole-wheat flour
- 4 tbsp non-hydrogenated vegetable shortening
- 1 tbsp sugar
- 2/3 cup low-fat milk
- 1 cup unbleached all-purpose flour
- 4 tsp sodium-free baking powder

Directions:
1. Preheat oven to 450°F. Whisk together white whole-wheat flour, unbleached all-purpose flour, sugar, and sodium-free baking powder in a mixing bowl.
2. Cut in the non-hydrogenated vegetable shortening using a fork or your fingers until it resembles coarse crumbs.
3. Whisk the egg white and low-fat milk in a separate bowl, add to the dry ingredients, and mix until a dough forms.
4. Knead the dough for 1 minute, roll it out to 3/4-inch thickness, and cut it into circles using a cookie cutter.
5. Bake the circles on the baking sheet for 10 minutes or until lightly golden.
6. Finally, cool the cookies on a cooling rack.

Nutritional Info Per Serving:
Calories: 140, Fats: 6 g
Carbs: 18 g, Proteins: 4 g
Potassium: 172mg, Sodium: 290 mg

Bean Frittata

Prep time: 5 minutes

Cook time: 16 minutes

Servings: 4

Ingredients:
- 4 eggs, beaten
- 1/2 cup low-sodium canned red kidney beans, rinsed and drained
- 1/2 onion, diced
- 1 tbsp. margarine
- 1 tsp. dried dill

Directions:
1. Place the margarine in the skillet. Add onion and sauté for 4 minutes or until it is soft.
2. Add dried dill and red kidney beans and mix.
3. Pour the eggs and cover.
4. Cook the frittata on medium-low heat until it is set or for 7 minutes, or bake for 5 minutes in the oven at 350°F.
5. Serve and enjoy.

Nutritional Info Per Serving:
Calories: 160, Fats: 8 g
Carbs: 9 g, Proteins: 12 g
Potassium: 310mg, Sodium: 120 mg

Buckwheat Crepes

Prep time: 8 minutes

Cook time: 5 minutes

Servings: 6

Ingredients:
- 1 cup buckwheat flour
- 1/3 cup whole grain flour
- 1 egg, beaten
- 1 cup skim milk
- 1 tsp. olive oil
- ½ tsp. ground cinnamon

Directions:
1. Mix all ingredients and whisk to form a smooth batter.
2. Heat a non-stick skillet.
3. Use a ladle to scoop a small amount of batter and flatten it to form a crepe shape. Put it into the skillet and cook each side for a minute and turn.
4. Repeat to finish all batter.

Nutritional Info Per Serving:
Calories: 122, Fats: 2.2 g
Carbs: 21 g, Proteins: 5.7 g
Potassium: 1357mg, Sodium: 221 mg

Cereal with Cranberry Orange Twist

Prep time: 5 minutes

Cook time: 0 minutes

Servings: 2

Ingredients:
- ½ cup water
- ½ cup unsweetened orange juice
- 1/3 cup oat bran
- ¼ cup dried cranberries
- Skim milk
- Stevia or different sugar substitute

Directions:
1. Combine all ingredients in a bowl.
2. Microwave the bowl for 2 minutes, and serve with skim milk and stevia or different sugar substitute.

Nutritional Info Per Serving:
Calories: 170, Fats: 2 g
Carbs: 39 g, Proteins: 4 g
Potassium: 260 mg, Sodium: 10 mg

Whole Grain Pancakes

Prep time: 5 minutes

Cook time: 2 minutes

Servings: 4

Ingredients:
- ½ tsp. baking powder
- ¼ cup skim milk
- 1 cup whole-grain wheat flour
- 2 tsp. liquid honey
- 1 tsp. olive oil

Directions:
1. In a mixing bowl, combine flour and baking powder.
2. Add skim milk and olive oil. Whisk the mixture well.
3. Preheat a non-stick skillet. Get a small piece of dough and shape it to a pancake and place it on the skillet. Cook each side for two minutes or until golden brown. Repeat until dough is finished.
4. Top with liquid honey.

Nutritional Info Per Serving:
Calories: 129, Fats: 1.7 g
Carbs: 25.7 g, Proteins: 4.6 g
Potassium: 785 mg, Sodium: 32 mg

Mediterranean Toast

Prep time: 10 minutes

Cook time: 0 minutes

Servings: 2

Ingredients:
- 1 1/2 tsp. reduced-Fat crumbled feta
- 3 sliced Greek olives
- 1/4 mashed avocado
- 1 slice multi grain bread
- 1 tbsp. red pepper hummus roasted
- 3 sliced cherry tomatoes
- 1 sliced hardboiled egg
- Black pepper

Directions:
1. Toast the bread and top with 1 tbsp. of hummus and mashed avocado.
2. Add the cherry tomatoes, olives, feta, and hardboiled egg.
3. Season with pepper to taste.

Nutritional Info Per Serving:
Calories: 334, Fats: 17 g
Carbs: 33.3 g, Proteins: 16.3 g
Potassium: 765mg, Sodium: 440 mg

Raspberry Yogurt

Prep time: 5 minutes

Cook time: 0 minutes

Servings: 2

Ingredients:
- ½ cup low-fat yogurt

- ½ cup raspberries
- 1 tsp. almond flakes

Directions:
1. Mix up raspberries and yogurt and transfer them to serving glasses.
2. Top yogurt with almond flakes.

Nutritional Info Per Serving:
Calories: 77, Fats: 3.4 g
Carbs: 8.6 g, Proteins: 3.9 g
Potassium: 416 mg, Sodium: 90 mg

Instant Banana Oatmeal

Prep time: 3 minutes

Cook time: 2 minutes

Servings: 1

Ingredients:
- 1 mashed ripe banana
- ½ cup. water
- ½ cup. quick oats

Directions:
1. Add water and oats into a microwave-safe bowl. Combine the mixture well.
2. Put the mixture in the microwave and heat for 2 minutes on high.
3. Remove from microwave, add the mashed banana, and stir.

Nutritional Info Per Serving:
Calories: 243, Fats: 3 g
Carbs: 50 g, Proteins: 6 g
Potassium: 454 mg, Sodium: 6 mg

Dash Apple Pancakes

Prep time: 10 minutes

Cook time: 10 minutes

Servings: 4

Ingredients:
- 1/4 cup extra-virgin olive oil, divided
- 1 cup whole wheat flour
- 2 tsp. baking powder
- 1 tsp. baking soda
- 1 tsp. ground cinnamon
- 1 cup skim milk
- 2 large egg whites
- 1 medium Gala apple, diced
- 2 tbsp. pure maple syrup
- 1/4 cup chopped unsalted walnuts

Directions:
1. Set aside 1 tsp. of oil to use for greasing a griddle or skillet. In a large bowl, stir the baking powder, flour, baking soda, cinnamon, egg whites, apple, and the remaining oil together.
2. Heat a griddle or skillet over medium-high heat and coat with the reserved oil. Working in batches, pour in about 1/4 cup of the batter for each pancake. Cook for 5 minutes until browned on both sides.

3. Place 4 pancakes into each of 4 medium storage containers and the maple syrup in 4 small containers.
4. To serve, sprinkle each serving with walnuts and drizzle with 1/2 tbsp. of maple syrup.

Nutritional Info Per Serving:
Calories: 316, Fats: 12 g
Carbs: 43 g, Proteins: 9 g
Potassium: 295mg, Sodium: 312 mg

Scallions Omelet

Prep time: 10 minutes

Cook time: 7 minutes

Servings: 2

Ingredients:
- 1 oz. scallions, chopped
- 2 eggs, beaten
- 1 tbsp. low-fat sour cream
- 1/4 tsp. ground black pepper
- 1 tsp. olive oil

Directions:
1. Heat up olive oil in the skillet.
2. Add the remaining ingredients to a mixing bowl and mix.
3. Pour the mixture into the skillet, flatten well, and cook for 7 minutes over medium-low heat.
4. Serve and enjoy.

Nutritional Info Per Serving:
Calories: 101, Fats: 8 g
Carbs: 1.8 g, Proteins: 6 g
Potassium: 465mg, Sodium: 264 mg

French Toast with Applesauce

Prep time: 5 minutes

Cook time: 3 minutes

Servings: 6

Ingredients:
- 1/4 cup unsweetened applesauce
- 1/2 cup skim milk
- 2 packets Stevia
- 2 eggs
- 6 slices whole-grain bread
- 1 tsp. ground cinnamon
- 1 tbsp. sugar

Directions:
1. Mix well applesauce, sugar, cinnamon, milk, eggs, and Stevia together.
2. One slice at a time, soak to wet the bread into the applesauce mixture.
3. Heat a large nonstick skillet on medium heat.
4. Add the bread slices and cook for 2-3 minutes on each side in a single layer in batches until lightly brown.
5. Serve immediately.

Nutritional Info Per Serving:
Calories: 122, Fats: 2.6 g
Carbs: 18.3 g, Proteins: 6.5 g
Potassium: 547mg, Sodium: 259 mg

Carrot Cake Overnight Oats

Prep time: 8 minutes

Cook time: 0 minutes

Servings: 1

Ingredients:
- ½ cup rolled oats
- ½ cup low-fat Greek yogurt
- ½ cup low-fat milk
- ¼ cup carrot, shredded
- 2 tbsp. raisins
- ½ tsp. ground cinnamon
- 1 to 2 tbsp. walnuts, chopped

Directions:
1. Mix all of the fixings in a jar and cover, shake well, and refrigerate overnight. Serve.

Nutritional Info Per Serving:
Calories: 331, Fats: 3 g
Carbs: 59 g, Proteins: 22 g
Potassium: 748mg, Sodium: 622mg

Egg Toasts

Prep time: 5 minutes

Cook time: 4 minutes

Servings: 3

Ingredients:
- 3 eggs
- 3 slices of whole-grain bread
- 1 tsp. olive oil
- ¼ tsp. minced garlic
- ¼ tsp. ground black pepper

Directions:
1. Heat up olive oil in the skillet.
2. Crack the eggs and cook until ready, for about 4 minutes.
3. In the meantime, rub minced garlic on the bread slices.
4. Top the eggs on the bread and drizzle some ground black pepper.

Nutritional Info Per Serving:
Calories: 157, Fats: 7.4 g
Carbs: 13.5 g, Proteins: 8.6 g
Potassium: 790mg, Sodium: 776 mg

Smoked Salmon Egg Scramble with Chives and Dill

Prep time: 5 minutes

Cook time: 6 minutes

Servings: 2

Ingredients:
- 1 tbsp. milk
- 1 tbsp. fresh chives, minced
- 4 large eggs
- ⅛ tsp. freshly ground black pepper
- 1 tbsp. fresh dill, minced
- ¼ tsp. kosher salt
- 2 tsp. extra-virgin olive oil
- 2 oz. smoked salmon, thinly sliced

Directions:
1. Whisk together chives, eggs, milk, dill, salt, and pepper in a large bowl.

2. Heat the olive oil in a medium skillet or sauté pan over medium heat. Add the egg mixture and cook for about 3 minutes, stirring occasionally.
3. Add the salmon and cook until the eggs are set but moist, about 1 minute.

Nutritional Info Per Serving:
Calories: 325, Fats: 6 g
Carbs: 1 g, Proteins: 23 g
Potassium: 300mg, Sodium: 455mg

Peach Pancakes

Prep time: 10 minutes

Cook time: 2 minutes

Servings: 6

Ingredients:
- 1 cup whole-wheat flour
- 1 egg, beaten
- 1 tsp. vanilla extract
- 2 peaches, chopped
- 1 tbsp. margarine
- ½ tsp. baking powder
- 1 tsp. apple cider vinegar
- ¼ cup skim milk

Directions:
1. Pancake batter: mix whole-wheat flour, apple cider vinegar, eggs, baking powder, vanilla extract, and skim milk in the mixing bowl.
2. Melt the margarine in the skillet.
3. Pour the prepared batter into the skillet with the help of the ladle and flatten in the shape of the pancake.
4. Cook each side for 2 minutes over medium-low heat.
5. Top the cooked pancakes with peaches.

Nutritional Info Per Serving:
Calories: 129, Fats: 3 g
Carbs: 21.5 g, Proteins: 3.9 g
Potassium: 947mg, Sodium: 138 mg

Apple Oats

Prep time: 5 minutes

Cook time: 7 minutes

Servings: 2

Ingredients:
- ½ cup oats
- 1 cup water
- 1 apple, chopped
- 1 tsp. olive oil
- ½ tsp. vanilla extract

Directions:
1. Add olive oil to a saucepan, and then add oats. Cook while stirring for 2 minutes.
2. Add water and stir.
3. Cover and cook for 5 minutes on low heat.
4. Add vanilla extract and chopped apples. Stir the meal.

Nutritional Info Per Serving:
Calories: 159, Fats: 3.9 g
Carbs: 29.4 g, Proteins: 3 g
Potassium: 464 mg, Sodium: 9 mg

Banana & Cinnamon Oatmeal

Prep time: 5 minutes

Cook time: 4 minutes

Servings: 6

Ingredients:
- 2 cups quick-cooking oats
- 4 cups unsweetened almond milk
- 1 tsp. ground cinnamon
- 2 chopped large ripe banana
- 4 tsp. brown sugar substitute (such as Stevia or Splenda)

Directions:
1. Add almond milk to a skillet and bring to a boil. Put in oats and cook for 4 minutes over medium heat.
2. Stir occasionally. Add cinnamon, banana, and brown sugar substitute, and stir. Serve and enjoy!

Nutritional Info Per Serving:
Calories: 170, Fats: 3g
Carbs: 32g, Proteins: 5g
Potassium: 225mg, Sodium: 95mg

Curry Tofu Scramble

Prep time: 7 minutes

Cook time: 3 minutes

Servings: 3

Ingredients:
- 12 oz. tofu, crumbled
- 1 tsp. curry powder
- ¼ cup skim milk
- 1 tsp. olive oil
- ¼ tsp. chili flakes

Directions:
1. Heat up olive oil in the skillet.
2. Add crumbled tofu and chili flakes.
3. Mix skim milk and curry powder in a bowl.
4. Pour milk mixture over the tofu and stir.
5. Cook tofu on medium-high heat for 3 minutes.

Nutritional Info Per Serving:
Calories: 102, Fats: 6.4 g
Carbs: 3.3 g, Proteins: 10 g
Potassium: 624mg, Sodium: 102mg

Steel-Cut Oatmeal with Plums and Pear

Prep time: 15 minutes

Cook time: 20 minutes

Servings: 4

Ingredients:
- 2 cups of water
- 1 cup nonfat or low-fat milk
- 1 cup steel-cut oats

- 1 cup dried plums, chopped
- 1 medium pear, cored, and skin removed, diced
- 4 tbsp. almonds, roughly chopped

Directions:
1. Combine the oats, milk, and water in a medium-sized pot and boil over high heat. Reduce the heat and cover. Simmer for about 10 minutes, stirring occasionally.
2. Add the plums and pear, and cover. Simmer for another 10 minutes.
3. Finally, turn off the heat and leave for 5 minutes to absorb all the liquid.
4. To serve, top each portion with a sprinkling of almonds.

Nutritional Info Per Serving:
Calories: 280, Fats: 7 g
Carbs: 47 g, Proteins: 9 g
Potassium: 697 mg, Sodium: 47 mg

Sweet Yogurt with Figs

Prep time: 5 minutes

Cook time: 0 minutes

Servings: 1

Ingredients:
- 1/3 cup yogurt, low-fat
- 1 tsp. almond flakes
- 1 chopped fresh fig
- 1 tsp. liquid honey
- 1/4 tsp. sesame seeds

Directions:
1. Mix honey and yogurt and pour the mixture into the serving glass.
2. Top it with sesame seeds, chopped fig, and almond flakes.

Nutritional Info Per Serving:
Calories: 178, Fats: 6.8 g
Carbs: 24.4 g, Proteins: 6.2 g
Potassium: 198 mg, Sodium: 39 mg

Sweet Potatoes with Coconut Flakes

Prep time: 15 minutes

Cook time: 1 hour

Servings: 2

Ingredients:
- 16 oz. sweet potatoes, peeled
- 1 tbsp. maple syrup
- 1/4 cup. Greek yogurt, fat-free coconut
- 1/8 cup. unsweetened toasted coconut flakes
- 1 apple, chopped

Directions:
1. Preheat oven to 400°F.
2. Put the potatoes on a baking sheet. Bake until soft or about 50 minutes.
3. Use a knife that is sharp to mark "X" on the potatoes and use a fork to fluff pulp.
4. Top with maple syrup, Greek yogurt, chopped apple, and coconut flakes.

5. Serve immediately.

Nutritional Info Per Serving:
Calories: 321, Fats: 3 g
Carbs: 70 g, Proteins: 7 g
Potassium: 2581mg, Sodium: 83 mg

Southwest Tofu Scramble

Prep time: 10 minutes

Cook time: 14 minutes

Servings: 1

Ingredients:
- ½ tbsp. olive oil
- ½ red onion, chopped
- 2 cups chopped spinach
- 8 oz. firm tofu, drained well
- 1 tsp. ground cumin
- ½ tsp. garlic powder
- Sliced avocado, sliced tomatoes

Directions:
1. Heat olive oil in a medium skillet. Add the onion and cook for about 5 minutes or until softened,
2. Add the spinach and cover to steam for 2 minutes.
3. Using a spatula, move the veggies to one side of the pan. Crumble the tofu into the open area in the pan, breaking it up with a fork.
4. Add the garlic and cumin to the crumbled tofu and mix well. Sauté for 5 to 7 minutes until the tofu is slightly browned.

5. Serve immediately with whole-grain bread, fruit, or beans. Top with sliced avocado and tomato.

Nutritional Info Per Serving:
Calories: 267, Fats: 0 g
Carbs: 13 g, Proteins: 23 g
Potassium: 1666mg, Sodium: 84 mg

Greek Yogurt Oat Pancakes

Prep time: 15 minutes

Cook time: 5 minutes

Servings: 2

Ingredients:
- 6 egg whites
- 1 cup rolled oats
- 1 cup plain nonfat Greek yogurt
- 1 medium banana, peeled and sliced
- 1 tsp. ground cinnamon
- 1 tsp. baking powder

Directions:
1. Blend all of the listed fixing using a blender. Warm a griddle over medium heat. Spray the skillet with nonstick cooking spray.
2. Put 1/3 cup of the mixture or batter onto the griddle. Allow to cook and flip when bubbles on the top burst, about 5 minutes.

3. Cook again within a minute until golden brown. Repeat with the remaining batter.
4. Divide between two serving plates and enjoy.

Nutritional Info Per Serving:
Calories: 318, Fats: 4 g
Carbs: 47 g, Proteins: 28 g
Potassium:1793mg, Sodium:338 mg

No-Cook Overnight Oats

Prep time: 5 minutes

Cook time: 30 minutes

Servings: 1

Ingredients:
- 1 ½ cup low-fat milk
- 5 whole almond pieces
- 1 tsp. chia seeds
- 2 tbsps. Oats
- 1 tsp. sunflower seeds
- 1 tbsp. raisins

Directions:
1. In a jar or mason bottle with a cap, mix all ingredients. Refrigerate overnight.
2. Enjoy for breakfast.

Nutritional Info Per Serving:
Calories: 271, Fats: 9.8 g
Carbs: 35 g, Proteins: 16.7 g
Potassium:227mg, Sodium: 1547mg

Avocado Cup with Egg

Prep time: 5 minutes

Cook time: 20 minutes

Servings: 4

Ingredients:
- 4 tsp. grated parmesan cheese
- 1 chopped stalk scallion
- 4 dashes black pepper
- 4 dashes paprika
- 2 ripe avocados
- 4 medium eggs

Directions:
1. Preheat the oven to 375°F.
2. Slice avocados in half and discard the seed.
3. Slice the rounded portions of avocados to make them level and place them on a baking sheet.
4. Crack an egg into each avocado hole on the baking sheet.
5. Season with paprika and black pepper.
6. Bake in preheated oven for 20 minutes or until eggs are cooked.
7. Sprinkle with grated parmesan before serving.

Nutritional Info Per Serving:
Calories: 206, Fats: 15.4 g
Carbs: 11.3 g, Proteins: 8.5 g
Potassium:3360mg, Sodium:527mg

Blueberry-Oatmeal Muffin in a Mug

Prep time: 2 minutes
Cook time: 1 minute
Servings: 1

Ingredients:
- 1/2 cup rolled oats
- 1 egg
- 2 tbsp. nonfat or low-fat milk
- 1/3 cup blueberries
- Cooking spray
- No-calorie sweetener of choice

Directions:
1. Spray a large mug or small ramekin with cooking spray.
2. Add the oats, egg, and milk, and stir to combine. Gently fold in the blueberries.
3. Place in the microwave and cook on high for 1 minute, being careful to watch as it could overflow. If the muffin does not look firm, place it back in the microwave for 30 seconds at a time.
4. Once ready, flip the mug upside down onto a plate. Slice, and enjoy.

Nutritional Info Per Serving:
Calories: 259, Fats: 8 g
Carbs: 36 g, Proteins: 13 g
Potassium: 507mg, Sodium: 123 mg

Stuffed Breakfast Peppers

Prep time: 10 minutes
Cook time: 35 minutes
Servings: 4

Ingredients:
- 4 bell peppers
- 1 bag frozen spinach
- 4 eggs
- 1/4 cup shredded low-fat cheese
- Freshly ground black pepper to taste

Directions:
1. Preheat the oven to 400°F. Line a baking dish with aluminum foil. Cut the tops off the peppers, then discard the tops and seeds. Put the peppers in the baking dish, and bake for about 15 minutes.
2. While the peppers bake, defrost the spinach and drain the excess moisture. Remove the peppers, then stuff the bottoms evenly with the defrosted spinach.
3. Crack an egg over the spinach inside each pepper. Top each egg with a tbsp. of the cheese (if using) and season with black pepper to taste.
4. Bake for 15 to 20 minutes or until the egg whites are set and opaque.

Nutritional Info Per Serving:
Calories: 136, Fats: 5 g
Carbs: 15 g, Proteins: 11 g
Potassium:1260mg, Sodium: 679mg

Breakfast Splits

Prep time: 15 minutes

Cook time: 0 minutes

Servings: 2

Ingredients:
- 2 bananas, peeled
- 4 tbsp. low-fat granola
- 2 tbsp. low-fat yogurt
- ½ tsp. ground cinnamon
- 1 strawberry, chopped

Directions:
1. In a mixing bowl, mix strawberries, ground cinnamon, and yogurt.
2. Cut the bananas lengthwise and fill them with the mixture.
3. Top with low-fat granola.

Nutritional Info Per Serving:
Calories: 193, Fats: 3 g
Carbs: 44 g, Proteins: 3 g
Potassium: 400 mg, Sodium: 26 mg

Savory Yogurt Bowls

Prep time: 15 minutes

Cook time: 0 minutes

Servings: 4

Ingredients:
- 1 medium cucumber, diced
- ½ cup pitted Kalamata olives, halved
- 2 tbsp. fresh lemon juice
- 1 tbsp. extra-virgin olive oil
- 1 tsp. dried oregano
- ¼ tsp. freshly ground black pepper
- 2 cups nonfat plain Greek yogurt
- ½ cup slivered almonds

Directions:
1. In a small bowl, mix the cucumber, olives, lemon juice, olive oil, oregano and pepper.
2. Divide the yogurt evenly among 4 storage containers. Top with the cucumber-olive mix and almonds.

Nutritional Info Per Serving:
Calories: 240, Fats: 16 g
Carbs: 10 g, Proteins: 16 g
Potassium: 332mg, Sodium: 619 mg

Coconut Crepes

Prep time: 10 minutes

Cook time: 3 minutes

Servings: 5

Ingredients:
- 1 cup almond flour
- 1 tbsp. ground flaxseed
- 2 cups unsweetened coconut milk
- 2 tbsp. coconut oil melted
- 1 tsp. cinnamon powder
- 2 tsp. stevia

Directions:
1. In a bowl, combine the flaxseed, almond flour, coconut milk, half of the coconut oil, cinnamon, and stevia, and mix well.
2. Heat a pan with the remaining coconut oil over medium heat, add ¼ cup of the batter, spread into the pan, cook for 2-3 minutes per side, and transfer to a plate.
3. Repeat with the rest of the batter to make crepes and serve for breakfast with desired DASH-friendly toppings like fruit, low-fat yogurt, or unsweetened cocoa powder.

Nutritional Info Per Serving:
Calories: 145, Fats: 12 g
Carbs: 7 g, Proteins: 3 g
Potassium: 125 mg, Sodium: 6 mg

Apple-Apricot Brown Rice Breakfast Porridge

Prep time: 15 minutes
Cook time: 3 minutes
Servings: 4

Ingredients:
- 3 cups cooked brown rice
- 1¾ cups nonfat or low-fat milk
- 2 tbsp. lightly packed brown sugar
- 4 dried apricots, chopped
- 1 medium apple, cored and diced
- ¾ tsp. ground cinnamon
- ¾ tsp. vanilla extract

Directions:
1. Combine the rice, milk, sugar, apricots, apple, and cinnamon in a medium saucepan.
2. Boil it on medium heat, reduce the heat down slightly, and cook within 2 to 3 minutes. Turn it off, then stir in the vanilla extract.
3. Serve warm.

Nutritional Info Per Serving:
Calories: 260, Fats: 2 g
Carbs: 57 g, Proteins: 7 g
Potassium: 620mg, Sodium:1813mg

Quinoa Bowl

Prep time: 15 minutes
Cook time: 15 minutes
Servings: 4

Ingredients:
- 2 cups water
- 1 cup quinoa
- 1 cup tomatoes, diced
- 1 cup sweet pepper, diced
- ½ cup rice, cooked
- 1 tbsp. olive oil
- 1 tbsp. lemon juice
- ½ tsp. grated lemon zest

⌧ Directions:
1. Mix quinoa and water and cook for about 15 minutes. Remove from heat set aside to rest for 10 minutes.
2. Put the quinoa in a big bowl.
3. Add rice, sweet pepper, olive oil, lemon juice, lemon zest, and tomatoes.
4. Stir well and transfer to serving bowls.

Nutritional Info Per Serving:
Calories: 290, Fats: 4 g
Carbs: 49.9 g, Proteins: 8.4 g
Potassium: 435 mg, Sodium: 11 mg

Appetizers, Snacks, and Sides

Turmeric Endives

Prep time: 10 minutes

Cook time: 20 minutes

Servings: 4

Ingredients:
- 2 endives, halved lengthwise
- 2 tbsp. olive oil
- 1 tsp. rosemary, dried
- ½ tsp. turmeric powder
- A pinch black pepper

Directions:
1. Mix the endives with the oil and the other ingredients in a baking pan, toss gently, and bake at 400°F within 20 minutes.
2. Serve as a side dish.

Nutritional Info Per Serving:
Calories: 64, Fats: 7.1 g
Carbs: 0.8 g, Proteins: 0.2 g
Potassium: 47 mg, Sodium: 1 mg

Lemon Asparagus

Prep time: 10 minutes

Cook time: 20 minutes

Servings: 4

Ingredients:
- 1 lb. asparagus, trimmed
- 2 tbsp. basil pesto
- 1 tbsp. lemon juice
- A pinch black pepper
- 3 tbsp. olive oil
- 2 tbsp. cilantro, chopped

Directions:
1. Arrange the asparagus in a lined baking sheet, add the pesto and the other ingredients, toss, and bake at 400°F for 20 minutes.
2. Serve as a side dish.

Nutritional Info Per Serving:
Calories: 114, Fats: 10.7 g
Carbs: 4.5 g, Proteins: 2.6 g
Potassium: 278 mg, Sodium: 4 mg

Creamy Broccoli Cheddar Rice

Prep time: 15 minutes

Cook time: 37 minutes

Servings: 6

Ingredients:
- 1 cup brown rice
- 2 cups chicken broth, low-sodium
- 1 onion, minced
- 3 tbsp. extra virgin olive oil, divided
- 2 garlic cloves, minced
- 1/2 cup skim milk
- 1/4 tsp. black pepper, ground
- 1/2 cups broccoli, chopped
- 1 cup cheddar cheese, low-sodium, shredded

Directions:
1. Put 1 tbsp. of the extra virgin olive oil in a large pot and sauté the onion plus garlic over medium heat within 2 minutes.
2. Put the chicken broth in a pot and wait for it to come to a boil before adding the rice. Simmer the rice over low heat for 25 minutes.
3. Stir the skim milk, black pepper, and remaining 2 tbsp. of olive oil into the rice. Simmer again within 5 more minutes.
4. Stir in the broccoli and cook the rice for 5 more minutes, until the broccoli is tender. Stir in the rice and serve while warm.

Nutritional Info Per Serving:
Calories: 200, Fats: 3 g
Carbs: 33 g, Proteins: 10 g
Potassium: 176 mg, Sodium: 400mg

Stuffed Sweet Potatoes

Prep time: 5 minutes

Cook time: 17 minutes

Servings: 2

Ingredients:
- ½ cup unsalted pistachios
- 1 lime juice
- 2 tsp. grated Parmesan cheese
- 1 tsp. balsamic vinegar
- 2 medium orange flesh sweet potatoes, washed
- 2 tsp. olive oil
- 10 oz. broccoli florets
- 2 tsp. minced garlic
- 2 tbsp. sun-dried tomatoes, chopped
- Black pepper to taste
- 2 sprigs fresh basil

Directions:
1. In a high-powered blender, blitz the pistachios, lime juice, Parmesan, and balsamic vinegar, until fine and sticky. Set aside.
2. Prick the sweet potatoes with a fork a few times, then cook them in the microwave for about 7-12 minutes. Time will vary according to the potato sizes. Once cooked, let rest for 5 minutes before cutting lengthways down the center and opening them up.
3. Fry the broccoli florets in the olive oil for about 2 minutes, then add the garlic and fry for another minute. Add the pistachio mixture and the sun-dried tomatoes and cook for another 3 minutes until the tomatoes have softened.
4. Stuff each potato with half of the stuffing mixture, and serve hot, garnished with a sprig of basil and black pepper.

Nutritional Info Per Serving:
Calories: 409, Fats: 19 g
Carbs: 52 g, Proteins: 13 g
Potassium: 1366mg, Sodium:139mg

Chili Broccoli

Prep time: 10 minutes

Cook time: 30 minutes

Servings: 4

Ingredients:
- 2 tbsp. olive oil
- 1-lb. broccoli florets
- 2 garlic cloves, minced
- 2 tbsp. chili sauce
- 1 tbsp. lemon juice
- A pinch black pepper
- 2 tbsp. cilantro, chopped

Directions:
1. In a baking pan, combine the broccoli with the oil, garlic, and the other, toss a bit, and bake at 400°F for 30 minutes.
2. Divide the mix between plates and serve as a side dish.

Nutritional Info Per Serving:
Calories: 108, Fats: 7.4 g
Carbs: 8.3 g, Proteins: 3.4 g
Potassium: 305 mg, Sodium: 153mg

No-Mayo Potato Salad

Prep time: 15 minutes

Cook time: 20 minutes

Servings: 8

Ingredients:
- 3 lb. red potatoes
- 1/2 cup extra virgin olive oil
- 5 tbsp. white wine vinegar, divided
- 2 tsp. Dijon mustard
- 1 cup red onion, sliced
- ½ tsp. black pepper, ground
- 2 tbsp. basil, fresh, chopped
- 2 tbsp. dill weed, fresh, chopped
- 2 tbsp. parsley, fresh, chopped

Directions:
1. Add the red potatoes to a large pot and cover them with water until the water level is 2 inches above the potatoes. Put the pot on high heat, then boil potatoes until they are tender when poked with a fork, about 15 to 20 minutes. Drain off the water.
2. Let the potatoes to cool until they can easily be handled but are still warm, then cut it in half and put them in a large bowl. Stir in 3 tbsp. of the white wine vinegar, giving the potatoes a good stir so that they can evenly absorb the vinegar.

3. Mix the rest of 2 tbsp. of vinegar, extra virgin olive oil, Dijon mustard, and black pepper in a small bowl. Add this mixture to the potatoes and give them a good toss to thoroughly coat the potatoes.
4. Toss in the red onion and minced herbs. Serve at room temperature or chilled. Serve immediately or store in the fridge for up to 4 days.

Nutritional Info Per Serving:
Calories: 144, Fats: 7 g
Carbs: 19 g, Proteins: 2 g
Potassium: 843mg, Sodium: 164 mg

Parmesan Endives

Prep time: 15 minutes

Cook time: 20 minutes

Servings: 4

Ingredients:
- 4 endives, halved lengthwise
- 1 tbsp. lemon juice
- 1 tbsp. lemon zest, grated
- 2 tbsp. fat-free parmesan, grated
- 2 tbsp. olive oil
- A pinch black pepper

Directions:
1. In a baking dish, combine the endives with the lemon juice and the other ingredients except for the parmesan and toss.
2. Sprinkle the parmesan on top, bake the endives at 400°F for 20 minutes, and serve.

Nutritional Info Per Serving:
Calories: 71, Fats: 7.1 g
Carbs: 2.2 g, Proteins: 0.9 g
Potassium: 61 mg, Sodium: 30 mg

Sweet Potatoes and Apples

Prep time: 15 minutes

Cook time: 40 minutes

Servings: 4

Ingredients:
- 2 sweet potatoes, sliced
- 2 apples
- 3 tbsp. extra virgin olive oil, divided
- 1/4 tsp. black pepper, ground
- 1 tsp. cinnamon, ground
- 2 tbsp. maple syrup

Directions:
1. Heart the oven to 425°F and grease a large baking sheet with non-stick cooking spray. Toss the cubed sweet potatoes with 2 tbsp. of the olive oil and black pepper until coated. Roast the potatoes within 20 minutes, stirring them

once halfway through the process.
2. Meanwhile, toss the apples with the remaining tbsp. of olive oil, cinnamon, and maple syrup until evenly coated. After the sweet potatoes have cooked for 20 minutes, add the apples to the baking sheet and toss the sweet potatoes and apples.
3. Return to the oven, then roast it for 20 more minutes, once again giving it a good stir halfway through. Once the potatoes and apples are caramelized from the maple syrup, remove them from the oven and serve hot.

Nutritional Info Per Serving:
Calories: 100, Fats: 0 g
Carbs: 22 g, Proteins: 2 g
Potassium: 127 mg, Sodium: 92 mg

Coconut, Strawberries, and Chocolate

Prep time: 15 minutes

Cook time: 0 minutes

Servings: 2

Ingredients:
- 3 oz. 70% dark chocolate, chopped finely
- 1/3 cup unsweetened coconut milk
- 1/2 tsp. orange zest
- 12 strawberries, stalks and leaves removed

Directions:
1. Place the chocolate in a medium glass bowl.
2. Heat the coconut milk in a small pot until it just starts to steam, then add the orange zest and pour it over the chocolate.
3. Let the mixture sit for about 3 minutes, then stir well until the chocolate is fully melted and the mixture is smooth.
4. Serve the strawberries with a ramekin of the sauce to dip them in.

Nutritional Info Per Serving:
Calories: 149, Fats: 10 g
Carbs: 16 g, Proteins: 3 g
Potassium: 316 mg, Sodium: 2 mg

Roasted Turnips

Prep time: 10 minutes

Cook time: 30 minutes

Servings: 4

Ingredients:
- 2 cups turnips, peels, and cut into 1/2" cubes
- 1/4 tsp. black pepper, ground
- 1/2 tsp. garlic powder
- 1/2 tsp. onion powder
- 1 tbsp. extra virgin olive oil

Directions:
1. Warm the oven to 400°F and prepare a large baking sheet, setting it aside. Begin by trimming the top and bottom edges off of the turnips and peeling them if you wish. Slice them into ½-inch cubes.
2. Toss the turnips with the extra virgin olive oil and seasonings, and then spread them out on the prepared baking sheet.
3. Roast the turnips until tender, stirring them halfway through, about 30 minutes in total.

Nutritional Info Per Serving:
Calories: 50, Fats: 4 g
Carbs: 5 g, Proteins: 1 g
Potassium: 187 mg, Sodium: 46 mg

Balsamic Cabbage

Prep time: 15 minutes

Cook time: 15 minutes

Servings: 4

Ingredients:
- 1 lb. green cabbage, roughly shredded
- 2 tbsp. olive oil
- A pinch black pepper
- 1 shallot, chopped
- 2 garlic cloves, minced
- 2 tbsp. balsamic vinegar
- 2 tsp. hot paprika
- 1 tsp. sesame seeds

Directions:
1. Heat-up a pan with the oil over medium heat, add the shallot and the garlic, and sauté for 5 minutes.
2. Add the cabbage and the other ingredients, toss, cook over medium heat for 15 minutes, divide between plates and serve.

Nutritional Info Per Serving:
Calories: 100, Fats: 7.5 g
Carbs: 8.2 g, Proteins: 1.8 g
Potassium: 306mg, Sodium: 317 mg

Avocado, Tomato, and Olives Salad

Prep time: 5 minutes

Cook time: 0 minutes

Servings: 4

Ingredients:
- 2 tbsp. olive oil
- 2 avocados, cut into wedges
- 1 cup Kalamata olives, pitted and halved
- 1 cup tomatoes, cubed
- 1 tbsp. ginger, grated
- A pinch black pepper
- 2 cups baby arugula
- 1 tbsp. balsamic vinegar

Directions:
1. Combine the Kalamata olives with avocados and the other ingredients in a bowl. Toss and serve as a side dish.

Nutritional Info Per Serving:
Calories: 320, Fats: 30.4 g
Carbs: 13.9 g, Proteins: 3 g
Potassium: 664mg, Sodium: 261 mg

Peanut and Chocolate Squares

Prep time: 10 minutes

Cook time: 25 minutes

Servings: 9

Ingredients:
- ½ cup dehydrated peanut butter powder
- 2 tbsp. unsweetened, natural peanut butter
- 15 oz. cooked chickpeas, drained and rinsed
- ¼ cup rolled oats
- ¼ cup unsweetened almond milk
- ¼ cup butternut squash puree
- ¼ cup stevia
- 2 tsp. vanilla extract
- ¾ tsp. baking powder
- ⅛ tsp. baking soda
- Canola oil spray
- 2 tbsp. dark chocolate chips

Directions:
1. Preheat the oven to 350°F.
2. Using a high-powered blender, blend the peanut butter powder, natural peanut butter, chickpeas, oats, almond milk, butternut squash puree, stevia, vanilla extract, baking powder, and baking soda until a thick, smooth batter is formed.
3. Spray an 8 x 8-inch baking dish with canola oil spray, and then pour the batter into it.
4. Sprinkle the dark chocolate chips over the top and press them down lightly.
5. Bake in the oven for about 25 minutes, or until cooked all the way through.
6. Place the tray on a cooling rack and allow it to cool completely before cutting into equal squares.
7. Enjoy!

Nutritional Info Per Serving:
Calories: 104, Fats: 3 g
Carbs: 13 g, Proteins: 6 g
Potassium: 322 mg, Sodium: 95 mg

Simple Pear Crumble

Prep time: 5 minutes

Cook time: 35 minutes

Servings: 6

Ingredients:
- 5 pears, peeled, cored, and cut into large dice
- 2 tbsp. honey
- 1 tbsp. lime juice
- 2 tbsp. corn flour
- ½ tsp. cinnamon powder
- Flavorless oil in a spray bottle
- 1 cup homemade Granola

⌧ **Directions:**
1. Place the pears, honey, lime juice, corn flour, and cinnamon in a bowl and mix well.
2. Preheat the oven to 350°F.
3. Oil an 11 by 8 ½ inch baking dish lightly, add the pear mixture, bake for 30 minutes, and stir once halfway through the baking.
4. Sprinkle the granola over the top of the pears and return to the oven. Bake for a further 5 minutes. Remove from the oven and allow to rest for 5 minutes.
5. Serve hot and enjoy.

Nutritional Info Per Serving:
Calories: 201, Fats: 5 g
Carbs: 38 g, Proteins: 4 g
Potassium: 15 mg, Sodium: 0 mg

Spanish rice

Prep time: 15 minutes

Cook time: 1 hour 18 minutes

Servings: 8

Ingredients:
- 2 cups brown rice
- 1/4 cup extra virgin olive oil
- 2 garlic cloves, minced
- 1 onion, diced
- 2 tomatoes, diced
- 1 jalapeno, seeded and diced
- 1 tbsp. tomato paste
- 1/2 cup cilantro, chopped
- 1/2 cups chicken broth

⌧ **Directions:**
1. Warm the oven to 375°F. Puree the tomatoes, onion, plus garlic using a blender or food processor. Measure out 2 cups of this vegetable puree to use and discard the excess.
2. Into a large oven-safe Dutch pan, heat the extra virgin olive oil over medium heat until hot and shimmering. Add in the jalapeno and rice to toast, cooking while occasionally stirring for 2 to 3 minutes.
3. Slowly stir the chicken broth into the rice, followed by the vegetable puree and tomato paste. Stir until combine and increase the heat to medium-high until the broth reaches a boil.
4. Cover the Dutch pan with an oven-safe lid, transfer the pot to the preheated oven, and bake within 1 hour and 15 minutes. Remove and stir the cilantro into the rice. Serve.

Nutritional Info Per Serving:
Calories: 265, Fats: 3 g
Carbs: 40 g, Proteins: 5 g
Potassium: 143mg, Sodium: 124 mg

Cilantro Lime Rice

Prep time: 15 minutes

Cook time: 30 minutes

Servings: 6

Ingredients:
- 1.5 cups brown rice
- 2 tbsp. lime juice
- 1.5 tsp. lemon juice
- 1/2 tsp. lime zest
- 1/4 cup cilantro, chopped
- 1 bay leaf
- 1 tbsp. extra virgin olive oil
- Water

Directions:
1. Cook rice and bay leaf in a pot with boiling water. Mix and allow it to boil for 30 minutes, reducing the heat slightly if need be.
2. Once the rice is tender, drain off the water, and return the rice to the pot. Let it sit off of the heat within 10 minutes. Remove bay leaf and fluff the rice with a fork.
3. Stir the rest of the fixing into the rice and then serve immediately.

Nutritional Info Per Serving:
Calories: 94, Fats: 3 g
Carbs: 15 g, Proteins: 2 g
Potassium: 12 mg, Sodium: 20 mg

Lime Carrots

Prep time: 10 minutes

Cook time: 30 minutes

Servings: 4

Ingredients:
- 1 lb. baby carrots, trimmed
- 1 tbsp. sweet paprika
- 1 tsp. lime juice
- 1 tbsp. extra virgin olive oil
- A pinch black pepper
- 1 tsp. sesame seeds

Directions:
1. Preheat the oven to 400°F. Line a baking sheet with parchment paper.
2. Combine the carrots, paprika, lime juice, olive oil, and black pepper in a mixing bowl. Toss well to coat.
3. Place the carrots in a single layer on the baking sheet.
4. Roast in the oven for approximately 30 minutes or until the carrots are tender.
5. Sprinkle the carrots with sesame seeds before serving.

Nutritional Info Per Serving:
Calories: 70, Fats: 4 g
Carbs: 8 g, Proteins: 1 g
Potassium: 250 mg, Sodium: 61 mg

Choco-Fudge Cookies

🍴 *Prep time: 10 minutes*

🍳 *Cook time: 15 minutes*

🍽 *Servings: 12*

Ingredients:
- 15 oz. cooked chickpeas, rinsed and drained
- 3 tbsp. smooth pecan nut butter
- ½ cup cocoa powder, unsweetened
- ½ cup rolled oats
- ¼ cup pumpkin puree
- 1 tsp. vanilla essence
- 1 tsp. cinnamon
- 1 tsp. baking powder
- ¼ cup stevia
- 2 tbsp. almond milk
- 6 tbsp. egg whites
- Canola oil in a spray bottle

Directions:
1. Preheat the oven to 350°F.
2. Using a high-powered blender, blend the chickpeas, pecan nut butter, cocoa powder, rolled oats, pumpkin puree, vanilla essence, cinnamon, baking powder, stevia, almond milk, egg whites, and honey to form a smooth cookie dough.
3. Lightly grease a baking sheet with canola oil spray. Spoon out 12 cookies onto the sheet. Press them down slightly and then bake for about 15 minutes, or until firm.
4. Let cool and serve.

Nutritional Info Per Serving:
Calories: 65, Fats: 1 g
Carbs: 12 g, Proteins: 5 g
Potassium: 293 mg, Sodium: 24 mg

Very-Berry Mug Cake

🍴 *Prep time: 10 minutes*

🍳 *Cook time: 4 minutes*

🍽 *Servings: 3*

Ingredients:
- ¼ tsp. canola oil, plus extra in a spray bottle
- 2 tbsp. low-fat sour cream
- 2 tbsp. low-fat almond milk
- 1 large egg white
- ½ tsp. almond extract
- 3 cherries, pitted and diced
- 1 strawberry, diced
- ¼ cup whole wheat pastry flour
- 1 ½ tsp. stevia powder
- ¼ tsp. baking powder

Directions:
1. In a small bowl, mix the ¼ tsp. oil, sour cream, almond milk, egg white,

almond extract, cherries, and strawberry. Set aside.
2. In another small bowl, mix the flour, stevia, and baking powder.
3. Whisk together the two bowls of ingredients to form a smooth cake batter.
4. Lightly spray a microwave-safe mug with canola oil, then pour the cake batter into it.
5. Microwave on high for 3-4 minutes, or until cooked.
6. As soon as the mug comes out of the microwave, run a knife around the edges to loosen the cake. Flip upside-down over a serving plate and remove from the mug.
7. Allow to cool before serving.

Nutritional Info Per Serving:
Calories: 109, Fats: 2 g
Carbs: 16 g, Proteins: 6 g
Potassium: 89 mg, Sodium: 77 mg

Zesty Yogurt Pots

Prep time: 15 minutes

Cook time: 0 minutes

Servings: 2

Ingredients:
- 2 oz. low-fat mascarpone, at room temperature
- ½ cup low-fat yogurt
- 2 ½ tbsp. lime juice, plus lime zest to garnish
- 2 tsp. honey
- 4 digestive biscuits
- Ready-made whipped cream to serve

Directions:
1. Place the mascarpone, yogurt, lime juice, and honey in a bowl and whisk well to combine.
2. In a high-powered blender, blitz the biscuits to a large crumb size, then press these crumbs into the bottoms of two dessert ramekins.
3. Spoon the yogurt mixture into the ramekins, smoothing over the top.
4. Put in the fridge to set for an hour.
5. Serve chilled, topped with whipped cream, and garnished with lime zest.

Nutritional Info Per Serving:
Calories: 219, Fats: 13 g
Carbs: 18 g, Proteins: 8 g
Potassium: 391mg, Sodium: 925 mg

Spinach and Endives Salad

Prep time: 5 minutes

Cook time: 0 minutes

Servings: 4

Ingredients:
- 2 endives, roughly shredded
- 1 tbsp. dill, chopped
- ¼ cup lemon juice

- ¼ cup olive oil
- 2 cups baby spinach
- 2 tomatoes, cubed
- 1 cucumber, sliced
- ½ cups walnuts, chopped

Directions:
1. Combine In a large bowl, the endives with the spinach and the other ingredients, toss and serve as a side dish.

Nutritional Info Per Serving:
Calories: 238, Fats: 22.3 g
Carbs: 8.4 g, Proteins: 5.7 g
Potassium: 311 mg, Sodium: 16 mg

Butternut Squash Apple Salad

Prep time: 15 minutes

Cook time: 30 minutes

Servings: 3

Ingredients:
- 2 tsp. olive oil
- A butternut squash, seeded and peeled, cut into ½ inch pieces
- 2 big apples, cored and cut ½-inch pieces
- 2 cups chopped carrots
- 1½ cups chopped celery
- 6 cups spinach, chopped
- 6 cups arugula, chopped

Dressing:
- ½ cup low-fat plain yogurt
- 2 tsp. balsamic vinegar
- 1½ tsp. honey

Directions:
1. Heat oven to 400°F. Stir squash in olive oil, roast in the oven for 20-30 minutes until golden and tender. Let it cool completely.
2. Mix all the vegetables in a large bowl. Prepare the vinaigrette by mixing yogurt, vinegar, and honey. Beat until smooth. Pour the vinaigrette over the salad.
3. Toss and serve immediately.

Nutritional Info Per Serving:
Calories: 334, Fats: 9g
Carbs: 47g, Proteins: 19g
Potassium: 1080mg, Sodium: 97 mg

Italian Roast Mushrooms

Prep time: 5 minutes

Cook time: 30 minutes

Servings: 4

Ingredients:
- 2 tbsp. olive oil
- 10 oz pink oyster mushrooms
- Black pepper to taste
- 1 tsp. fresh basil, chopped
- 1 tsp. fresh thyme, finely chopped
- 1 sprig rosemary
- 2 tbsp. garlic, finely sliced

Directions:
1. Preheat the oven to 400ºF.
2. Oil a baking tray, add all the ingredients except the garlic to the tray. Toss well to coat the mushrooms fully.
3. Roast in the oven for about 25 minutes. Remove from the oven, and layer the garlic beneath the mushrooms, and roast for an additional 5 minutes.
4. Serve hot and enjoy.

Nutritional Info Per Serving:
Calories: 94, Fats: 7 g
Carbs: 5 g, Proteins: 2 g
Potassium: 1148 mg, Sodium: 11 mg

Apple Blue Cheese Salad

Prep time: 15 minutes

Cook time: 0 minutes

Servings: 4

Ingredients:
- 3 apples, peeled, cored, and cubed
- 1 tbsp. lemon juice
- 1 cup plain low-fat or nonfat yogurt, preferable Greek-style
- ¼ tsp. cayenne pepper
- ½ tsp. black pepper
- 1/3 cup blue cheese crumbled
- 1/3 cup pistachios

Directions:
1. Add the apples to a bowl and sprinkle with lemon juice. Add yogurt and pepper to apples and toss to combine. Put in the refrigerator and let cool for at least 30 minutes.
2. When about to serve, add blue cheese and pistachios and mix well.

Nutritional Info Per Serving:
Calories: 200, Fats: 8 g
Carbs: 25 g, Proteins: 8.5 g
Potassium: 433mg, Sodium: 172 mg

Spiced Fruity Cookies

Prep time: 10 minutes

Cook time: 10 minutes

Servings: 12

Ingredients:
- 1 very ripe banana
- 1/4 cup smooth almond butter
- 2 tbsp. honey
- 2 tbsp. canola oil, plus extra in a spray bottle
- 1 large egg
- 1/4 cup rolled oats
- 1/2 tsp. vanilla extract
- 1/2 cup whole wheat flour
- 1/4 tsp. baking powder
- 1/4 tsp. cinnamon
- 1/8 tsp. cloves
- 1/8 tsp. nutmeg
- 1/4 cup pecan nuts, roughly chopped

Directions:

1. Preheat the oven to 350°F.
2. In a mixing bowl, mash the banana and mix in almond butter, honey, and canola oil. Add the egg, rolled oats, and vanilla extract, mix well.
3. In a separate bowl, sift together the flour, baking powder, cinnamon, cloves, and nutmeg. Add the chopped nuts and mix.
4. Combine the wet and dry ingredients to form a firm cookie dough.
5. Roll out balls using your hands. Then place them on a well-oiled baking sheet and press down to form cookies.
6. Bake for 8-10 minutes, or until the edges are lightly golden. Remove from the oven and allow the cookies to cool on a wire rack.

Nutritional Info Per Serving:
Calories: 116, Fats: 6.2 g
Carbs: 13.8 g, Proteins: 2.9 g
Potassium: 98 mg, Sodium: 13 mg

Roasted Brussels Sprouts

Prep time: 15 minutes

Cook time: 30 minutes

Servings: 6

Ingredients:
- 2 lb Brussels sprouts
- 3 garlic cloves, minced
- 3 tbsp. balsamic vinegar
- 1/4 cup extra virgin olive oil
- ½ tsp. black pepper, ground
- 1/2 cup parmesan cheese, low-sodium, grated

Directions:

1. Preheat your oven to 425°F.
2. Remove the yellow leaves and stems from the Brussels sprouts and cut them in half.
3. In a large bowl, mix together minced garlic, black pepper, balsamic vinegar, and extra virgin olive oil. Add the Brussels sprouts and toss until they are evenly coated.
4. Spread the Brussels sprouts evenly on a large baking sheet lined with parchment paper.
5. Roast the Brussels sprouts for 25-30 minutes in the preheated oven, stirring them halfway through, until they are tender and lightly browned.
6. Sprinkle the Brussels sprouts with grated Parmesan cheese after removing them from the oven. Return the baking sheet to the oven and bake for another 3-5 minutes, until the cheese is melted and bubbling.
7. Serve the roasted Brussels sprouts hot.

Nutritional Info Per Serving:
Calories: 119, Fats: 7 g
Carbs: 12g, Proteins: 6 g
Potassium: 460mg, Sodium: 142 mg

Garlic Potato Pan

Prep time: 10 minutes

Cook time: 50 minutes

Servings: 5

Ingredients:
- 1 lb. gold potatoes, peeled and cut into wedges
- 2 tbsp. olive oil
- 1 red onion, chopped
- 2 garlic cloves, minced
- 1 cup unsweetened coconut milk
- 1 tbsp. thyme, chopped
- ¼ tsp. nutmeg, ground
- ¼ cup low-fat parmesan, grated

Directions:
1. Heat a pan with the oil over medium heat, put the onion plus the garlic, and sauté for 5 minutes. Add the potatoes and brown them for 5 minutes more.
2. Add the coconut milk, thyme, nutmeg, and parmesan cheese, toss gently, bring to a simmer and cook over medium heat for 40 more minutes or until the potatoes are cooked through.
3. Divide the mixture between plates and serve as a side dish.

Nutritional Info Per Serving:
Calories: 196, Fats: 10.9 g
Carbs: 21.6 g, Proteins: 3.5 g
Potassium: 606mg, Sodium: 126 mg

Moist Chocolate Brownies

Prep time: 15 minutes

Cook time: 30 minutes

Servings: 9

Ingredients:
- 2 large eggs
- ½ cup cocoa powder
- 2/3 cup caster sugar
- 14 oz. cooked black beans, rinsed and drained
- 3 tbsp. olive oil
- ½ tsp. baking powder
- ½ cup chocolate chips
- 2 tbsp. pecan nut pieces
- Canola oil in a spray bottle

Directions:
1. Preheat the oven to 350°F.
2. Place all the ingredients, except for ¼ cup chocolate chips and the pecan nuts, in a high-powered blender, and blend on high to form a smooth batter.
3. Lightly oil an 8 by 8-inch baking tin, and pour the brownie mixture into it. Scatter the remaining chocolate chips and pecans over the top.
4. Bake in the oven for about 30 minutes, or until just cooked.

5. Allow to cool before cutting into equal brownies and serving.

Nutritional Info Per Serving:
Calories: 214, Fats: 9 g
Carbs: 32 g, Proteins: 5 g
Potassium: 309 mg, Sodium: 4 mg

Arugula Salad

Prep time: 5 minutes

Cook time: 0 minutes

Servings: 4

Ingredients:
- ¼ cup pomegranate seeds
- 5 cups baby arugula
- 6 tbsp. green onions, chopped
- 1 tbsp. balsamic vinegar
- 2 tbsp. olive oil
- 3 tbsp. pine nuts
- ½ shallot, chopped

Directions:
1. Combine pomegranate, arugula and the rest of the ingredients in a salad bowl. Toss and serve.

Nutritional Info Per Serving:
Calories: 120, Fats: 11.6 g
Carbs: 4.2 g, Proteins: 1.8 g
Potassium: 158 mg, Sodium: 10 mg

Creamy Cauliflower Mash

Prep time: 10 minutes

Cook time: 25 minutes

Servings: 4

Ingredients:
- 2 lb. cauliflower florets
- ½ cup coconut milk
- A pinch black pepper
- ½ cup low-fat sour cream
- 1 tbsp. cilantro, chopped
- 1 tbsp. chives, chopped

Directions:
1. Put the cauliflower in a pot, add water to cover, bring to a boil over medium heat, and cook for 25 minutes and drain.
2. Mash the cauliflower, add the milk, black pepper, and cream, whisk well, divide between plates, sprinkle the rest of the ingredients on top, and serve.

Nutritional Info Per Serving:
Calories: 188, Fats: 13.4 g
Carbs: 15 g, Proteins: 6.1 g
Potassium: 873mg, Sodium: 181 mg

Zucchini Tomato Bake

Prep time: 10 minutes

Cook time: 30 minutes

Servings: 4

Ingredients:
- 10 oz. grape tomatoes, cut in half
- 2 zucchinis
- 5 garlic cloves, minced
- 1 tsp. Italian herb seasoning
- ¼ tsp. black pepper, ground

- ½ cup parsley, fresh, chopped
- ½ cup parmesan cheese, grated

Directions:
1. Heat the oven to 350°F and coat a large baking sheet with non-stick cooking spray. Mix the tomatoes, zucchini, garlic, Italian herb seasoning, Black pepper, and Parmesan cheese in a bowl.
2. Put the mixture out on the baking sheet and roast until the zucchini for 30 minutes. Remove, and garnish with parsley over the top before serving.

Nutritional Info Per Serving:
Calories: 35, Fats: 2 g
Carbs: 4 g, Proteins: 2 g
Potassium: 242mg, Sodium: 232mg

Paprika Brussels sprouts

Prep time: 10 minutes

Cook time: 25 minutes

Servings: 4

Ingredients:
- 2 tbsp. olive oil
- 1 lb. Brussels sprouts, trimmed and halved
- 3 green onions, chopped
- 2 garlic cloves, minced
- 1 tbsp. balsamic vinegar
- 1 tbsp. sweet paprika
- A pinch black pepper

Directions:
1. In a baking pan, combine the Brussels sprouts with the oil and the other ingredients, toss and bake at 400°F within 25 minutes.
2. Divide the mix between plates and serve.

Nutritional Info Per Serving:
Calories: 121, Fats: 7.6 g
Carbs: 12.6 g, Proteins: 4.4 g
Potassium: 613 mg, Sodium: 40 mg

Lunch Recipes

Tofu & Green Bean Stir Fry

Prep time: 15 minutes

Cook time: 10 minutes

Servings: 4

Ingredients:
- 1 14-oz. package extra-firm tofu
- 2 tbsp. canola oil
- 1-pound green beans, chopped
- 2 carrots, peeled and thinly sliced
- ½ cup stir fry sauce
- 2 cups fluffy brown rice
- 2 scallions, thinly sliced
- 2 tbsp. sesame seeds

Directions:
1. Put the tofu on your plate lined with a kitchen towel, put a separate kitchen towel over the tofu, and place a heavy pot on top, changing towels every time they become soaked. Rest for 15 minutes to remove the moisture. Cut the tofu into 1-inch cubes.
2. Heat canola oil in a large wok or skillet to medium-high heat. Add the tofu cubes and cook, flipping every 1 to 2 minutes, so all sides become browned. Remove from the skillet and place the green beans and carrots in the hot oil. Stir-fry for 4 to 5 minutes, occasionally tossing, until crisp and slightly tender.
3. While the vegetables are cooking, prepare the stir fry sauce (if using homemade). Place the tofu back in the skillet. Pour the sauce over the tofu and vegetables and let simmer for 2 to 3 minutes.
4. Serve over rice, then top with scallions and sesame seeds.

Nutritional Info Per Serving:
Calories: 380, Fats: 15 g
Carbs: 45 g, Proteins: 16 g
Potassium: 290mg, Sodium: 326 mg

Salmon and Edamame Cakes

Prep time: 10 minutes

Cook time: 30 minutes

Servings: 2

Ingredients:
- 4 cups flaked, cooked salmon
- 1 cup frozen Edamame, thawed
- 4 large egg whites
- 1/2 cup whole-wheat panko breadcrumbs (Japanese breadcrumbs)
- 2 scallions, finely chopped
- 2 tbsp. fresh ginger, peeled, minced
- 2 cloves garlic, crushed

- 2 tbsp. cilantro, finely chopped
- Canola oil cooking spray
- Lime wedges to serve

Directions:
1. Add all the ingredients except lime wedges to a bowl and mix well.
2. Divide the mixture into 8-10 balls and shape them into cakes.
3. Arrange the cakes on a plate lined with wax paper. Refrigerate the cakes for about 30 minutes.
4. Place a nonstick skillet over medium heat. Spray with cooking spray. When the skillet is heated, add 3-4 cakes.
5. Cook until the underside is golden brown. Flip and cook the other side. Both take 30 minutes.
6. Serve hot with lemon wedges and a dip of your choice.

Nutritional Info Per Serving:
Calories: 267, Fats: 13 g
Carbs: 5 g, Protein: 21 g
Potassium:1089mg, Sodium:239mg

Easy Salmon Steaks

Prep time: 10 minutes
Cook time: 18 minutes
Servings: 4

Ingredients:
- 1 large salmon fillet, cut into 4 steaks
- 3 garlic cloves, minced
- 1 yellow onion, chopped
- Black pepper to taste
- 2 tbsp. olive oil
- ¼ cup parsley, chopped
- Juice of 1 lemon
- 1 tbsp. thyme, chopped
- 4 cups of water

Directions:
1. Heat a pan with the oil on medium-high heat, cook onion and garlic for 3 minutes.
2. Add black pepper, parsley, thyme, water, and lemon juice, stir, bring to a gentle boil, add salmon steaks, cook them for 15 minutes, drain, divide between plates and serve with a side salad for lunch.

Nutritional Info Per Serving:
Calories: 350, Fats: 21 g
Carbs: 5 g, Proteins: 35 g
Potassium:1050mg, Sodium:105 mg

Cauliflower "Mac and Cheese" Casserole

Prep time: 15 minutes
Cook time: 45 minutes
Servings: 2

Ingredients:
- 5 cups cauliflower florets
- Sunflower seeds and pepper to taste
- 1 cup unsweetened almond milk
- 1/2 cup low-sodium vegetable broth
- 2 tbsp. whole wheat flour
- 1 beaten organic egg
- 1/2 cup grated reduced-fat cheddar cheese
- 1/4 cup grated Parmesan cheese
- 1/4 cup whole wheat panko bread crumbs

Directions:
1. Preheat your oven to 350 °F.
2. Season cauliflower florets with sunflower seeds and pepper and steam until firm.
3. Place the steamed cauliflower in a greased 8x8 inch ovenproof dish.
4. In a saucepan, heat almond milk over medium heat and season with sunflower seeds and pepper.
5. Stir in vegetable broth and whole wheat flour and cook until the sauce thickens.
6. Remove from heat and stir in beaten egg.
7. Pour the sauce over the cauliflower and mix in the grated cheddar and Parmesan cheese.
8. Sprinkle the bread crumbs on top of the cheese.
9. Bake for 30-45 minutes or until the top is golden brown and crispy.

Nutritional Info Per Serving:
Calories: 275, Fats: 13 g
Carbs: 22 g, Proteins: 20 g
Potassium: 839mg, Sodium:446 mg

Danish Style Duck with Cucumber and Carrots

Prep time: 10 minutes
Cook time: 40 minutes
Servings: 8

Ingredients:
- 1 duck, skin removed and cut up into medium pieces
- 1 cucumber, chopped
- 1 tbsp. low sodium vegetable stock
- 2 carrots, chopped
- 2 cups of water
- Black pepper as needed
- 1-inch ginger piece, grated

Directions:
1. Place small pieces of duck in a frying pan.
2. Cook over medium heat until the duck is browned on all sides. Add cucumber, stock, carrots, water, ginger, pepper and stir.
3. Bring the mixture to a boil, then reduce heat to

low and let simmer for 40 minutes.
4. Serve and enjoy!

Nutritional Info Per Serving:
Calories: 247, Fats: 8 g
Carbs: 6 g, Proteins: 36 g
Potassium: 431 mg, Sodium: 64 mg

Roasted Mushroom Risotto

Prep time: 10 minutes

Cook time: 1 hour 20 minutes

Servings: 4

Ingredients:
- 12 oz. sliced mushrooms
- 1 tsp. olive oil
- 1 tsp. Italian seasoning
- 4 cups low-sodium vegetable broth
- 1 cup Arborio rice
- 1/4 cup grated Parmesan cheese
- Salt and pepper to taste

Directions:
1. Preheat the oven to 400°F.
2. Toss sliced mushrooms with olive oil and Italian seasoning. Roast in the oven for 20 minutes, stirring occasionally.
3. In a large saucepan, bring vegetable broth to a simmer over medium heat.
4. Add Arborio rice and stir until fully coated with broth. Continue to stir frequently as the rice absorbs the liquid.
5. Add more broth as needed until the rice is fully cooked and creamy.
6. Stir in the roasted mushrooms and Parmesan cheese.
7. Season with salt and pepper to taste.
8. Serve and enjoy!

Nutritional Info Per Serving:
Calories: 240, Fats: 4 g
Carbs: 44 g, Proteins: 7 g
Potassium: 361 mg, Sodium:194 mg

Lentil Avocado Tacos

Prep time: 15 minutes

Cook time: 35 minutes

Servings: 6

Ingredients:
- 1 tbsp. canola oil
- ½ yellow onion, peeled and diced
- 2-3 garlic cloves, minced
- 1½ cups dried lentils
- ½ tsp. kosher or sea salt
- 3 cups unsalted vegetable stock
- 2½ tbsp. taco seasoning or store-bought low-sodium taco seasoning
- 16 (6-inch) corn tortillas, toasted
- 2 ripe avocados, peeled and sliced

✖ Directions:
1. Heat the canola oil in a large skillet or Dutch oven over medium heat. Cook the onion for 4 to 5 minutes, until soft.
2. Mix in the garlic and cook for 30 seconds until fragrant. Then add the lentils, salt, and stock.
3. Bring to a simmer for 25 to 35 minutes, adding additional stock if needed.
4. When there's only a small amount of liquid left in the pan, and the lentils are al dente, stir in the taco seasoning and let simmer for 1 to 2 minutes. Taste and adjust the seasoning, if necessary.
5. Spoon the lentil mixture into tortillas and serve with the avocado slices.

Nutritional Info Per Serving:
Calories: 400, Fats: 14 g
Carbs: 64 g, Proteins: 16 g
Potassium: 715mg, Sodium: 336 mg

Japanese Potato and Beef Croquettes

Prep time: 10 minutes

Cook time: 16 minutes

Servings: 2

Ingredients:
- 3 medium russet potatoes, peeled and chopped
- 1 tbsp. almond butter
- 1 tbsp. vegetable oil
- 3 onions, diced
- 3/4-pound lean ground beef
- 4 tsp. reduced-sodium soy sauce
- Whole wheat flour for coating • 2 eggs, beaten
- Whole wheat panko breadcrumbs for coating
- 1/2 cup olive oil, frying

✖ Directions:
1. Place a saucepan over medium-high heat; add potatoes and enough water to cover them, boil for 16 minutes.
2. Remove water and put potatoes in another bowl, add almond butter and mash the potatoes.
3. Place a frying pan over medium heat, add 1 tbsp. oil and let it heat up.
4. Add onions and stir fry until tender.
5. Add soy sauce to beef and onions.
6. Keep frying until beef is browned.
7. Mix the beef with the potatoes evenly.
8. Take another frying pan and place it over medium heat; add half a cup of olive oil.
9. Form croquettes using the mashed potato mixture and coat them with whole

wheat flour, then eggs and finally whole wheat panko breadcrumbs.
10. Fry patties until golden on all sides. Enjoy!

Nutritional Info Per Serving:
Calories: 418, Fats: 21 g
Carbs: 31 g, Proteins: 27 g
Potassium:1179mg, Sodium:439 mg

Avocado Sandwich with Lemon and Cilantro

Prep time: 10 minutes

Cook time: 0 minutes

Servings: 2

Ingredients:
- 1 medium Hass avocado
- 4 slices of 100% whole wheat bread
- 2 cups spinach
- 1/4 cup cilantro
- 1/2 cup shredded carrots
- 1/2 cup sliced cucumber
- 1 tbsp. lemon juice
- 1 cup skim milk

Directions:
1. Toast the bread.
2. Slice the avocado into thin strips and divide equally among the slices of toast.
3. Add a layer of spinach on top of the avocado slices.
4. Top each slice of toast with shredded carrots and sliced cucumber.
5. Sprinkle each slice with a splash of lemon juice.
6. Serve with a glass of skim milk.

Nutritional Info Per Serving:
Calories: 299, Fats: 11 g
Carbs: 43 g, Proteins: 11 g
Potassium: 822mg, Sodium: 273 mg

Paella with Chicken, Leeks, and Tarragon

Prep time: 15 minutes

Cook time: 20 minutes

Servings: 2

Ingredients:
- 2 tsp. olive oil, extra-virgin
- 1 large onion, sliced
- 4 leeks sliced thinly (whites only)
- 6 -7 minced garlic cloves
- 1 pound chicken breast, boneless, skinless
- 1 large tomato, chopped
- 1 sliced red pepper
- 1 green pepper, sliced
- 1 1/3 cups long-grain brown rice
- 2 tsp. tarragon, or to taste
- 2 cups unsalted chicken broth, fat-free
- 2 cups frozen peas
- 1/2 cup fresh parsley, chopped
- 2 lemons, cut into 4 wedges each

Directions:

1. Heat olive oil in a skillet. Once heated, sauté onions, garlic, leeks, and chicken for a few minutes or until the onions become translucent and the chicken is light brown.
2. Add tomatoes and peppers, then sauté for 4-5 minutes.
3. Add tarragon, broth and rice. Mix well.
4. Bring to a boil, then lower heat, cover, and simmer for about 12-15 minutes.
5. Uncover and add peas. Wait for it to simmer or until all the moisture is absorbed and rice is cooked.
6. Sprinkle parsley and serve with lemon wedges.

Nutritional Info Per Serving:
Calories: 378, Fats: 6 g
Carbs: 46 g, Proteins: 35 g
Potassium: 902mg, Sodium: 546mg

Balsamic Chicken and Vegetables

Prep time: 15 minutes

Cook time: 25 minutes

Servings: 2

Ingredients:
- 4 chicken thighs, boneless and skinless
- 5 stalks of asparagus, halved
- 1 pepper, cut into chunks
- 1/2 red onion, diced
- ½ cup carrots, sliced
- 1 garlic clove, minced
- 2 oz. of mushrooms, diced
- ¼ cup balsamic vinegar
- 1 tbsp. olive oil
- ½ tsp. stevia
- ½ tbsp. oregano
- Sunflower seeds and pepper as needed
- Salt-free seasoning blend

Directions:
1. Preheat your oven to 425°F.
2. Take a bowl and add all the vegetables and mix.
3. Add spices, salt-free seasoning blend, and oil and mix.
4. Dip the chicken pieces into a spice mix and coat them well.
5. Place the veggies and chicken onto a pan in a single layer.
6. Cook for 25 minutes.
7. Serve and enjoy!

Nutritional Info Per Serving:
Calories: 401, Fats: 17 g
Carbs: 11 g, Proteins: 48 g
Potassium: 1256mg, Sodium: 57 mg

Flat Bread Pizza

Prep time: 15 minutes

Cook time: 22 minutes

Servings: 3

Ingredients:
- 1 tbsp. of olive oil, plus topping if needed
- 1 lb. flatbread dough
- 1/2 tsp. of dried herbs, red pepper flakes, or other spices
- 1 bunch of fresh broccoli, cauliflower, arugula, or other leafy greens vegetables
- 1 bell pepper, diced

Directions:
1. Set the grill to medium heat and brush with a thin layer of oil
2. Cook the flatbread dough on both sides until golden brown, about 2 minutes on each side.
3. Top flatbread with vegetables. Season to taste with olive oil, pepper, red pepper flakes, or herbs.
4. To finish cooking, place flatbread pizza into the oven and bake for 20 minutes.
5. Serve and enjoy.

Nutritional Info Per Serving:
Calories: 130, Fats: 1 g
Carbs: 25 g, Proteins: 5 g
Potassium: 723mg, Sodium: 931 mg

Simple Veal Chops

Prep time: 10 minutes

Cook time: 17 minutes

Servings: 4

Ingredients:
- 3 tbsp. essential olive oil
- 1 grated, lemon zest
- 3 tbsp. whole-wheat flour
- 1½ cup. whole-wheat breadcrumbs
- Black pepper
- 1 tbsp. milk
- 4 veal rib chops
- 2 eggs

Directions:
1. Put whole-wheat flour in a bowl.
2. In a different bowl, mix milk with eggs and whisk
3. In 1/3 bowl, mix the breadcrumbs with lemon zest.
4. Season veal chops with black pepper, dredge them in flour, and dip them inside egg mix then in breadcrumbs.
5. Heat up a pan with the oil over medium-high heat, add veal chops, cook for 2 main minutes on both sides and transfer to a baking sheet. Place them inside the oven at 350°F, bake for a quarter-hour, divide between plates and serve with a side salad.
6. Enjoy!

Nutritional Info Per Serving:
Calories: 270, Fats: 6 g
Carbs: 10 g, Proteins: 16 g
Potassium: 123 mg, Sodium: 54 mg

Grilled Flank Steak with Lime Vinaigrette

Prep time: 10 minutes

Cook time: 15 minutes

Servings: 6

Ingredients:
- 2 tbsp. lime juice, freshly squeezed
- 2 tbsp. extra-virgin olive oil
- ½ tsp. ground black pepper
- ¼ cup chopped fresh cilantro
- 1 tbsp. ground cumin
- ¼ tsp. red pepper flakes
- ¾ pound flank steak

Directions:
1. Heat the grill to low medium heat
2. In a food processor, place all ingredients except for the cumin, red pepper flakes, and flank steak. Pulse until smooth. This will be the vinaigrette sauce. Set aside.
3. Season the flank steak with ground cumin and red pepper flakes and allow to marinate for at least 10 minutes.
4. Place the steak on the grill rack and cook for 5 minutes on each side. Cut into the center to check the doneness of the meat. You can also insert a meat thermometer to check the internal temperature.
5. Remove from the grill and allow to stand for 5 minutes.
6. Slice the steak into 2-inch strips and toss the vinaigrette to flavor the meat.
7. Serve with salad if desired.

Nutritional Info Per Serving:
Calories: 103, Fats: 5 g
Carbs: 1 g, Proteins: 13 g
Potassium: 241 mg, Sodium: 73 mg

Chicken Vegetable Soup

Prep time: 5 minutes

Cook time: 15 minutes

Servings: 2

Ingredients:
- 2 tbsp. olive oil
- 3 garlic cloves
- 1 onion
- 4 cups low sodium chicken broth
- 1/2 cup carrot, sliced
- 1/2 cup a parsnip, sliced
- 2 cups green collar, minced
- 1 can black beans, drained
- 1/2 cup seaweed

⌧ **Directions:**
1. Simmer olive oil, garlic, and onion.
2. Add the broth and vegetables to the chicken and boil for 10 minutes.
3. Lower to a simmer.
4. Simmer until the vegetables are soft.
5. Pour in the strained canned beans and optional seaweed when 5 minutes left to cook.

Nutritional Info Per Serving:
Calories: 269, Fats: 14 g
Carbs: 24 g, Proteins: 15 g
Potassium: 918mg, Sodium: 253 mg

Sesame Breadsticks

Prep time: 10 minutes

Cook time: 20 minutes

Servings: 4

Ingredients:
- 1 egg white
- 2 tbsp. almond flour
- 1 tsp. Himalayan pink sunflower seeds
- 1 tbsp. extra-virgin olive oil
- ½ tsp. sesame seeds

⌧ **Directions:**
1. Preheat oven to 320°F.
2. In a bowl, whisk the egg white. Add almond flour, half of the sunflower seeds, and olive oil.
3. Knead the mixture until you have a smooth dough.
4. Divide the dough into 4 pieces and roll each piece into a breadstick.
5. Put the sticks on a baking sheet covered with parchment paper.
6. Brush the sticks with olive oil, sprinkle with sunflower seeds and sesame seeds.
7. Bake for 20 minutes.
8. Serve and enjoy!

Nutritional Info Per Serving:
Calories: 334, Fats: 9g
Carbs: 47g, Proteins: 19g
Potassium: 25mg, Sodium: 44mg

Spicy Chili Salmon with Lemon

Prep time: 10 minutes

Cook time: 7 minutes

Servings: 4

Ingredients:
- 4 salmon fillets, boneless and skin-on
- 2 tbsp. assorted chili peppers, chopped
- Juice of 1 lemon
- 1 lemon, sliced
- 1 cup low-sodium chicken broth
- ¼ tsp. black pepper

⌧ **Directions:**
1. Pour chicken broth into the Instant Pot.

2. Add a steamer basket and place salmon fillets on top.
3. Sprinkle chili peppers over the fillets and season with black pepper.
4. Drizzle lemon juice on top and add lemon slices.
5. Lock the lid and cook for about 7 minutes on HIGH pressure.
6. Release the pressure naturally over 10 minutes.
7. Divide the salmon and lemon slices between serving plates.

Nutritional Info Per Serving:
Calories: 226, Fats: 9 g
Carbs: 3 g, Proteins: 31 g
Potassium: 577 mg, Sodium: 110 mg

Chicken and Broccoli

Prep time: 15 minutes

Cook time: 20 minutes

Servings: 4

Ingredients:
- 1 tbsp. olive oil
- 4 chicken breasts, skinless and boneless
- 1 cup red onions, chopped
- 2 garlic cloves, minced
- 1 tbsp. oregano, chopped
- ½ cup coconut cream
- 2 cups broccoli florets

Directions:
1. Heat oil in a pan over high heat. Add in the chicken breasts and cook each side for 4 minutes.
2. Add onions and garlic, stir and cook for 5 minutes more.
3. Add oregano, broccoli, and cream, toss everything, cook for 10 minutes more, divide between plates and serve.
4. Enjoy!

Nutritional Info Per Serving:
Calories: 287, Fats: 10 g
Carbs: 14 g, Proteins: 19 g
Potassium: 805mg, Sodium: 192 mg

New York Strip Steak with Mushroom Sauce

Prep time: 15 minutes

Cook time: 11 minutes

Servings: 2

Ingredients:
- 2 New York Strip steaks, 4 oz. each, trimmed from fat
- 3 cloves of garlic, minced
- 2 oz. shiitake mushrooms, sliced
- 2 oz. button mushrooms, sliced
- ¼ tsp. thyme
- ¼ tsp. rosemary
- ½ cup low-sodium beef broth

Directions:
1. Heat the grill to 350°F.
2. Position the grill rack 6 inches from the heat source.

3. Grill the steaks for 10 minutes on each side or until slightly pink on the inside.
4. Meanwhile, prepare the sauce. In a small nonstick pan, water sauté the garlic, mushrooms, thyme, and rosemary for a minute. Pour in the broth and bring to a boil. Allow the sauce to simmer until the liquid is reduced.
5. Top the steaks with the mushroom sauce.
6. Serve with a side of grilled vegetables.
7. Enjoy!

Nutritional Info Per Serving:
Calories: 230, Fats: 7 g
Carbs: 6 g, Proteins: 30 g
Potassium: 745mg, Sodium: 102 mg

Zucchini Pad Thai

Prep time: 15 minutes

Cook time: 25 minutes

Servings: 2

Ingredients:

For the sauce:
- 3/4 tbsp. coconut sugar
- 1 tsp. Sriracha sauce or to taste
- 2 tbsp. tamarind paste
- 2 tsp. low sodium tamari
- 1 tbsp. lime juice
- 2 tbsp. low sodium chicken stock

For the noodles:
- 1 large carrot, peeled, trimmed
- 2 large zucchinis, trimmed

For Pad Thai:
- 1/2 cups bean sprouts
- 1 large skinless, boneless chicken breast, sliced
- 1 egg, beaten
- 2 tsp. olive oil, divided
- 1 green onion, thinly sliced
- 2 tbsp. peanuts, finely chopped
- Lime wedges to serve
- Pepper powder to taste

Directions:
1. To make noodles: Use a spiralizer or julienne peeler to make noodles out of the carrot and zucchini.
2. For the Pad Thai: Place a nonstick pan over medium heat. Add 1/2 tsp. oil. When the oil is heated, add egg, and pepper. Keep stirring to scramble it. Remove from the pan when cooked and place it in a bowl.
3. Put oil in a warm nonstick pan. Once heated, add chicken breasts, and pepper.
4. Cook for 20 minutes until the chicken is tender inside and golden-brown outside. Place it along with the egg.

5. To make the sauce: Add all the ingredients of the sauce to a bowl and mix well. Place the pan back on the heat. Put the sauce mixture into the pan and cook until it is bubbly.
6. Add zucchini and carrot noodles and sauté for 5 minutes until it is thoroughly heated and slightly softened.
7. Add chicken, eggs, and sprouts. Mix well and heat thoroughly.
8. Garnish with lemon wedges, green onion, and peanuts and serve immediately.

Nutritional Info Per Serving:
Calories: 224, Fats: 3 g
Carbs: 12 g, Proteins: 11 g
Potassium:2733mg, Sodium:459mg

Peppery Beef Tenderloin

Prep time: 10 minutes

Cook time: 30 minutes

Servings: 3

Ingredients:
- 2 tsp. chopped sage
- 2 tsp. chopped thyme
- 2 tsp. chopped rosemary
- 2 garlic cloves, sliced
- 4 tsp. olive oil
- Sunflower seeds and pepper to taste
- 2 ½ pounds beef tenderloin, trimmed of visible fat

Directions:
1. Preheat your oven to 425 º F.
2. Take a small knife and cut incisions in the tenderloin; insert one slice of garlic into the incision.
3. Rub meat with oil.
4. Take a bowl and add sunflower seeds, sage, thyme, rosemary, pepper and mix well.
5. Rub the spice mix over tenderloin.
6. Put rubbed tenderloin into the roasting pan and bake for 10 minutes.
7. Lower temperature to 350°F and cook for 20 minutes more until an internal thermometer reads 145 degrees F.
8. Transfer tenderloin to a cutting board and let sit for 15 minutes; slice into 20 pieces and enjoy!

Nutritional Info Per Serving:
Calories: 366, Fats: 20 g
Carbs: 1 g, Proteins: 43 g
Potassium: 524mg, Sodium: 127 mg

Red Beans and Rice

Prep time: 15 minutes

Cook time: 50 minutes

Servings: 2

Ingredients:
- ½ cup dry brown rice
- 1 cup water, plus ¼ cup
- 1 can red beans, drained
- 1 tbsp. ground cumin
- Juice of 1 lime
- 4 handfuls of fresh spinach

Toppings:
- Avocado, chopped tomatoes, Greek yogurt, onions

Directions:
1. Mix rice plus water in a pot and bring to a boil. Cover and reduce heat to a low simmer. Cook for 30 to 40 minutes or according to package directions.
2. Meanwhile, add the beans, ¼ cup of water, cumin, and lime juice to a medium skillet. Simmer for 5 to 7 minutes.
3. Once the liquid is mostly gone, remove from the heat and add the spinach. Cover and let spinach wilt slightly, 2 to 3 minutes. Mix in with the beans.
4. Serve beans with rice. Add toppings, if using.

Nutritional Info Per Serving:
Calories: 232, Fats: 2 g
Carbs: 41 g, Proteins: 13g
Potassium: 448mg, Sodium: 315 mg

Pork and Roasted Tomato Mix

Prep time: 10 minutes
Cook time: 15 minutes
Servings: 6

Ingredients:
- 1/2 cup chopped yellow onion
- 2 cups chopped zucchinis
- 1 lb. ground pork meat
- ¾ cup shredded low-fat cheddar cheese
- Black pepper
- 15 oz. no-salt-added, chopped and canned roasted tomatoes

Directions:
1. Heat a pan over medium-high heat, add pork, onion, black pepper, and zucchini, stir and cook for 7 minutes.
2. Add roasted tomatoes, stir, bring to a boil, cook over medium heat for 8 minutes, divide into bowls, sprinkle cheddar on the top, and serve.
3. Enjoy!

Nutritional Info Per Serving:
Calories: 270, Fats: 5 g
Carbs: 10 g, Proteins: 12 g
Potassium: 409mg, Sodium: 181 mg

Curried Chicken wrap

Prep time: 10 minutes

Cook time: 0 minutes

Servings: 2

Ingredients:
- 2 medium whole-wheat tortillas
- 1/3 cup cooked chicken breast, chopped
- 1 cup apple, chopped
- 1 tbsp. plain Greek yogurt
- 1 tsp. curry powder
- 1 cup raw baby carrots

Directions:
1. Mix together all the ingredients except tortillas.
2. Divide and place at the center of the tortillas.
3. Roll and serve.

Nutritional Info Per Serving:
Calories: 300, Fats: 4 g
Carbs: 46 g, Proteins: 22 g
Potassium: 572mg, Sodium: 340 mg

Healthy Vegetable Fried Rice

Prep time: 15 minutes

Cook time: 6 minutes

Servings: 4

Ingredients:

For the sauce:
- 1/3 cup garlic vinegar
- 1½ tbsp. dark molasses
- 1 tsp. onion powder

For the fried rice:
- 1 tsp. olive oil
- 2 lightly beaten whole eggs + 4 egg whites
- 1 cup frozen mixed vegetables
- 1 cup frozen Edamame
- 2 cups cooked brown rice

Directions:
1. Prepare the sauce by combining the garlic vinegar, molasses, and onion powder in a glass jar. Shake well.
2. Heat oil in a large wok or skillet over medium-high heat. Add eggs and egg whites, let cook until the eggs set, for about 1 minute.
3. Break up eggs with a spatula or spoon into small pieces. Add frozen mixed vegetables and frozen Edamame. Cook for 4 minutes, stirring frequently.
4. Add the brown rice and sauce to the vegetable-and-egg mixture. Cook for 5 minutes or until heated through. Serve immediately.

Nutritional Info Per Serving:
Calories: 210, Fats: 6 g
Carbs: 28 g, Proteins: 19g
Potassium: 1611mg, Sodium: 199mg

Roasted Brussels Sprouts, Chicken, and Potatoes

Prep time: 10 minutes
Cook time: 20 minutes
Servings: 2

Ingredients:
- 1/2-pound chicken breasts, boneless, skinless
- 1/2 cups Yukon gold potatoes or red potatoes
- 2 cups Brussels sprouts, trimmed, quartered
- 1/2 cup onions, diced
- 1/4 cup low-sodium chicken broth
- 1 tbsp. lemon juice
- 1/4 tsp. garlic powder
- 1 tsp. dried oregano
- 1 tsp. Dijon mustard
- 2 tbsp. Kalamata olives, quartered
- Freshly ground black pepper to taste
- Cooking spray

Directions:
1. Grease a baking sheet with cooking spray.
2. Place the chicken pieces, Brussels sprouts, potatoes, and onions in a large bowl.
3. Mix together in a small bowl: chicken broth, lemon juice, mustard, oregano, pepper, olives, and garlic powder and pour over the vegetables in the bowl.
4. Transfer the contents to the baking sheet.
5. Bake in a pre-heated oven at 400 degrees F for 20 minutes or until the chicken and potatoes are tender.
6. Stir a couple of times.
7. Remove from the oven. Mix well and serve.

Nutritional Info Per Serving:
Calories: 361, Fats: 10 g
Carbs: 37 g, Proteins: 32 g
Potassium: 2189mg, Sodium: 353mg

Spinach and Beef Meatballs

Prep time: 10 minutes
Cook time: 20 minutes
Servings: 4

Ingredients:
- 1/2 cup onion
- 4 garlic cloves
- 1 whole egg
- 1/4 tsp. oregano
- Pepper as needed
- 1-pound lean ground beef
- 10 oz. spinach

Directions:
1. Preheat your oven to 375 degrees F.
2. Take a bowl and mix in the rest of the ingredients, and roll into meatballs using your hands.
3. Transfer to a baking sheet and bake for 20 minutes.
4. Enjoy!

Nutritional Info Per Serving:
Calories: 200, Fats: 8 g
Carbs: 5 g, Proteins: 29 g
Potassium: 847mg, Sodium: 143 mg

Beef Pot Roast

Prep time: 10 minutes

Cook time: 1 hour 15 minutes

Servings: 4

Ingredients:
- 3 ½ pounds beef roast, trimmed of visible fat
- 4 oz. mushrooms, sliced
- 1 ½ cups low-sodium beef broth
- 1 oz. of low-sodium onion soup mix
- ½ cup low-fat Italian dressing

Directions:
1. Preheat oven to 300°F.
2. In a bowl, mix together the beef broth, onion soup mix, and Italian dressing.
3. In a roasting pan, place the beef roast and pour the broth mixture over it.
4. Add sliced mushrooms.
5. Cover the pan with foil and bake for 1 hour and 15 minutes, or until the beef is tender.
6. Remove the roast from the pan for 10 minutes and then slice.
7. Serve the sliced beef with the mushrooms and gravy.

Nutritional Info Per Serving:
Calories: 325, Fats: 10 g
Carbs: 8 g, Proteins: 50 g
Potassium: 867mg, Sodium: 420mg

Spicy Cabbage Dish

Prep time: 10 minutes

Cook time: 4 hours

Servings: 4

Ingredients:
- 2 yellow onions, chopped
- 10 cups red cabbage, shredded
- 1 cup plums, pitted and chopped
- 1 tsp. cinnamon powder
- 1 garlic clove, minced
- 1 tsp. cumin seeds
- ¼ tsp. cloves, ground
- 2 tbsp. red wine vinegar
- 1 tsp. coriander seeds
- ½ cup water

Directions:
1. Add cabbage, onion, plums, garlic, cumin, cinnamon, cloves, vinegar, coriander, and water to your Slow Cooker.
2. Stir well.
3. Place lid and cook on LOW for 4 hours.
4. Divide between serving platters.
5. Enjoy!

Nutritional Info Per Serving:
Calories: 197, Fats: 1 g
Carbs: 14 g, Proteins: 3 g
Potassium: 2724mg, Sodium: 320mg

Healthy Avocado Beef Patties

Prep time: 15 minutes

Cook time: 5 minutes

Servings: 2

Ingredients:
- 1 pound 85% lean ground beef
- 1 small avocado, pitted and peeled
- Fresh ground black pepper as needed

Directions:
1. Pre-heat and prepare your broiler to high.
2. Divide beef into two equal-sized patties.
3. Season the patties with pepper accordingly.
4. Broil the patties for 5 minutes on each side.
5. Transfer the patties to a platter.
6. Slice avocado into strips and place them on top of the patties and serve!

Nutritional Info Per Serving:
Calories: 468, Fats: 43 g
Carbs: 9 g, Proteins: 38 g
Potassium: 1206mg, Sodium:146mg

Simple Pork and Capers

Prep time: 10 minutes

Cook time: 11 minutes

Servings: 2

Ingredients:
- 8 oz. cubed pork
- 1 cup low-sodium chicken stock
- Black pepper
- 2 tbsps. organic extra virgin olive oil
- 1 minced garlic oil
- 2 tbsp. capers

Directions:
1. Heat up a pan with the oil over medium-high heat, add the pork, season with black pepper and cook for 4 minutes on both sides.
2. Add garlic, capers and stock, stir and cook for 7 minutes more.
3. Divide everything between plates and serve.
4. Enjoy!

Nutritional Info Per Serving:
Calories: 224, Fats: 12 g
Carbs: 12 g, Proteins: 10 g
Potassium: 506mg, Sodium: 305mg

Buffalo Chicken Lettuce Wraps

Prep time: 35 minutes

Cook time: 9 minutes

Servings: 2

Ingredients:
- 3 chicken breasts, boneless and cubed
- 20 leaves of butter lettuce
- 3/4 cup cherry tomatoes, halved

- 1 avocado, chopped
- 1/4 cup green onions, diced
- 1/2 cup Greek yogurt ranch dressing
- 3/4 cup hot sauce

Directions:
1. Take a mixing bowl and add chicken cubes and hot sauce, mix.
2. Place in the fridge and let it marinate for 30 minutes.
3. Preheat your oven to 400 degrees F.
4. Place coated chicken on a cookie pan and bake for 9 minutes.
5. Assemble lettuce serving bowls with equal amounts of lettuce, green onions, tomatoes, Greek yogurt ranch dressing, and cubed chicken.
6. Serve and enjoy!

Nutritional Info Per Serving:
Calories: 373, Fats: 13 g
Carbs: 18 g, Proteins: 46 g
Potassium:1258mg,Sodium:1750mg

Baked Whole Wheat Macaroni and Beef Casserole

Prep time: 10 minutes
Cook time: 30 minutes
Servings: 3

Ingredients:
- 1-pound extra-lean ground beef
- 2 large onions, diced
- 2 boxes (7 oz. each) of whole-wheat elbow macaroni, cooked according to instructions on the package
- 2 jars (15 oz. each) of no-salt-added spaghetti sauce
- 3/4 cup grated Parmesan cheese

Directions:
1. Preheat oven to 350°F.
2. In a large nonstick pan over medium heat, sauté onions until they become translucent. Add beef and cook until brown.
3. Add pasta and spaghetti sauce. Mix well and transfer into a greased baking dish.
4. Bake in preheated oven for about 30 minutes.
5. Serve garnished with Parmesan cheese.

Nutritional Info Per Serving:
Calories: 398, Fats: 11 g
Carbs: 42 g, Proteins: 32 g
Potassium: 754mg, Sodium: 313 mg

Veggie Sushi

Prep time: 10 minutes
Cook time: 15 minutes
Servings: 2

Ingredients:
- 3 cups brown rice
- 2 tbsp. rice wine vinegar
- 2 avocados, longitudinally cut
- 2 carrots, longitudinally sliced
- 1 cucumber, longitudinally sliced
- Ponzu sauce, to taste
- ½ cabbage

Directions:
1. Cook brown rice according to package instructions. Add rice wine vinegar. Allow the cooked rice to cool down.
2. When cool, spread rice uniformly on a bamboo sushi mat using a wooden spoon. Alternatively, dip your hands in a cold bowl of water and spread the rice with your fingertips. Then, top with a layer of avocado, cabbage, and slices of cucumber.
3. Using the mat, roll a packed roll of rice and vegetable, slide the mat out, and repeat.
4. Slice into circles of 1/2 inch. Serve.

Nutritional Info Per Serving:
Calories: 135, Fats: 3 g
Carbs: 22 g, Proteins: 3 g
Potassium: 2000mg, Sodium: 34mg

Almond Butternut Chicken

Prep time: 10 minutes
Cook time: 25 minutes
Servings: 4

Ingredients:
- ½ pound nitrate-free bacon
- 6 chicken thighs, boneless and skinless
- 2-3 cups almond butternut squash, cubed
- Extra virgin olive oil
- Fresh sage, chopped
- Sunflower seeds and pepper as needed

Directions:
1. Start by preheating your oven to 425°F.
2. Take a large skillet and place it over medium-high heat, add bacon and fry until crispy.
3. Take a slice of bacon and place it on the side, and then crumble the bacon.
4. Add cubed almond butternut squash in the bacon grease and sauté, season with sunflower seeds and pepper.
5. Once the squash is tender, remove skillet and transfer to a plate.
6. Add coconut oil to the skillet and add chicken thighs, cook for 10 minutes.

7. Season with sunflower seeds and pepper.
8. Remove skillet from stove and transfer to oven.
9. Bake for 12-15 minutes, top with the crumbled bacon and sage.
10. Enjoy!

Nutritional Info Per Serving:
Calories: 323, Fats: 19 g
Carbs: 8 g, Proteins: 12 g
Potassium: 994mg, Sodium: 621 mg

Cobb Salad

Prep time: 10 minutes

Cook time: 10 minutes

Servings: 2

Ingredients:
- 2 tbsp. extra virgin olive oil
- 2 boneless, skinless chicken breasts, halved
- 1/4 cup leftover roasted turkey breast
- 1 lb. head romaine lettuce, sliced, rinsed, and dried using a salad spinner
- 1 Small bunch of frisée, washed and dried using a salad spinner
- 1 medium avocado, pitted, peeled, and chopped
- 3 large eggs, hard-boiled and chopped into circles
- 1 tbsp. chopped mustard seed
- 1 tbsp. sliced fresh chives
- 1 tbsp. freshly squeezed lemon juice
- Freshly chopped black pepper

Directions:
1. Warm cooking oil in a cast-iron skillet over medium heat.
2. Pat the chicken breasts dry with paper towels and cook for 3-4 minutes on each side. Test for an internal temperature of 160 ° F using an instant-read thermometer. Remove from heat, arrange on a plate, loosely cover with foil, and put aside.
3. Add the diced turkey to the same pan and cook for 2 to 3 minutes, just enough to crisp. Remove the paper towels from the heat and rinse.
4. Mix the romaine and frisée, then divide equally between two large plates. Cut the chicken into small pieces and carefully place them on top.
5. Arrange the turkey, avocado, tomato, and chopped eggs over the lettuce in orderly rows.
6. Mix lemon juice, mustard seed, and chives in a small cup. Put the glaze on top of the salad, if desired, add with pepper.

Nutritional Info Per Serving:
Calories: 392, Fats: 23 g
Carbs: 21 g, Proteins: 32 g
Potassium: 1310mg, Sodium: 426mg

Baked Eggs in Avocado

Prep time: 10 minutes

Cook time: 15 minutes

Servings: 2

Ingredients:
- 2 avocados
- 2 limes Juice
- Freshly ground black pepper
- 4 eggs
- 2 8-inch whole wheat or corn tortillas, warmed

Optional for serving:
- Halved cherry tomatoes and chopped cilantro

Directions:
1. Adjust the oven rack to the middle position and preheat the oven to 450°F. Scrape out the center of halved avocado using a spoon about 1½ tbsp.
2. Press lime juice over the avocados and season with black pepper to taste, and then place it on a baking sheet. Crack an egg into the avocado.
3. Bake for 10 to 15 minutes. Remove and garnish with optional cilantro and cherry tomatoes and serve with warm tortillas.

Nutritional Info Per Serving:
Calories: 534, Fats: 39 g
Carbs: 30 g, Proteins: 19 g
Potassium:1337mg, Sodium: 219mg

Mediterranean Shrimp Pasta with Artichokes and Spinach

Prep time: 10 minutes

Cook time: 10 minutes

Servings: 2

Ingredients:
- 1 tbsp. extra-virgin olive oil
- 1 medium onion, diced small
- 1/2 cup mushrooms, thinly sliced
- 2 garlic cloves, thinly sliced
- 1/2 cup canned artichokes, quartered
- 1/2 cups low-sodium chicken broth
- 6-oz. whole wheat angel hair pasta, broken in half
- 1/2 cup raw shrimps, peeled, deveined
- 1/2 tsp. dried oregano
- 2 cups fresh spinach roughly chopped
- Pepper to taste
- A pinch of crushed red pepper flakes

⌧ **Directions:**
1. Place a pot with olive oil over medium heat. When the oil is heated, add onions, mushrooms, and garlic.
2. Sauté for 5 minutes and add artichokes, chicken broth, pasta, shrimps, oregano, red pepper flakes, and pepper.
3. Mix well and bring to a boil. Put the cover and cook until the pasta is al dente.
4. Add spinach and cook until it wilts or for about 5 minutes.
5. Adjust the seasonings if required. Serve hot.

Nutritional Info Per Serving:
Calories: 430, Fats: 11 g
Carbs: 59 g, Proteins: 27 g
Potassium:1040mg, Sodium:300mg

Artichoke Spinach Chicken

⅙ *Prep time: 7 minutes*

🍲 *Cook time: 15 minutes*

🥘 *Servings: 4*

Ingredients:
- 2 tbsp. olive oil
- 10 oz. baby spinach
- 14 oz. artichoke hearts, chopped
- 4 chicken breasts, boneless and skinless
- 28 oz. tomato sauce, no-salt-added
- ½ tsp. red pepper flakes, crushed

⌧ **Directions:**
1. Bring the pan to medium heat -high heat, add chicken and red pepper flakes, and cook for 5 minutes on each side.
2. Add spinach, artichokes, and tomato sauce, toss, cook for 10 minutes more, divide between plates, and serve.

Nutritional Info Per Serving:
Calories: 212, Fats: 3 g
Carbs: 16 g, Proteins: 20 g
Potassium: 564mg, Sodium: 290mg

Aromatic Spaghetti

⅙ *Prep time: 5 minutes*

🍲 *Cook time: 10 minutes*

🥘 *Servings: 3*

Ingredients:
- 1 tsp. dried basil
- ¼ cup soy milk
- 6 oz. whole-grain spaghetti
- 2 cups water
- 1 tsp. ground nutmeg

⌧ **Directions:**
1. First boil the water, then add the spaghetti and cook for 8 to 10 minutes. Meanwhile, boil the soy milk.

2. Drain the cooked spaghetti and mix it with soy milk, ground nutmeg, and dried basil.
3. Mix well and serve immediately.

Nutritional Info Per Serving:
Calories: 128, Fats: 1.5 g
Carbs: 25 g, Proteins: 5.5 g
Potassium: 245mg, Sodium: 16 mg

Open-Faced Garden Tuna Sandwich

Prep time: 10 minutes

Cook time: 15 minutes

Servings: 2

Ingredients:
- 2 cans low sodium tuna packed in water, drained
- 4 green onions, sliced
- 4 slices hearty multigrain bread
- 1 tbsp. fresh parsley chopped
- 1 tbsp. lemon juice
- 1 tbsp. extra-virgin olive oil
- 1/4 cup cherry tomatoes, sliced
- A handful of fresh arugula
- 2 tbsp. low-fat whipped cream cheese
- Black pepper powder to taste

Directions:
1. Mix oil, lemon juice, parsley, green onion, and pepper.
2. Add tuna to a bowl. Add about 2/3 of the above mixture and mix well.
3. Lightly spread some of the remaining mixture on both sides of the bread.
4. Heat a nonstick pan over high heat. Place the bread slices and cook until the bottom side is golden brown for about 15 minutes. Turn and cook the other side.
5. Add the remaining mixture to the arugula and toss well.
6. To make sandwiches: Spread cream cheese on each of the bread slices.
7. Divide and spread the tuna mixture over the slices. Place the arugula over the tuna mixture and, finally, cherry tomatoes.

Nutritional Info Per Serving:
Calories: 360, Fats: 20 g
Carbs: 18 g, Proteins: 24 g
Potassium: 965mg, Sodium: 1440mg

Chipotle Lettuce Chicken

Prep time: 10 minutes

Cook time: 30 minutes

Servings: 6

Ingredients:
- 1 pound chicken breast, cut into strips
- Splash of olive oil
- 1 red onion, finely sliced

- 14 oz. tomatoes
- 1 tsp. chipotle, chopped
- ½ tsp. cumin
- Lettuce as needed
- Fresh coriander leaves
- Jalapeño chilies, sliced
- Fresh tomato slices for garnish
- Lime wedges

Directions:
1. Heat oil in a non-stick frying pan.
2. Add chicken and cook until brown.
3. Keep the chicken on the side.
4. Add tomatoes, chipotle, cumin, coriander leaves, chilies and lime wedges to the same pan and simmer for 25 minutes until you have a nice sauce.
5. Add the chicken and cook for six minutes.
6. Transfer the mixture to a bowl.
7. Wrap the mixture with lettuce wraps and serve with a lemon squeeze.

Nutritional Info Per Serving:
Calories: 332, Fats: 15 g
Carbs: 13 g, Proteins: 34 g
Potassium: 327mg, Sodium: 82 mg

Easy Roasted Salmon

Prep time: 5 minutes
Cook time: 25 minutes
Servings: 2

Ingredients:
- 8 wild salmon fillets
- 2 lemons, cut into 8 wedges
- Freshly ground black pepper to taste
- 1/2 cup fresh dill, minced
- 8 cloves garlic, peeled and minced

Directions:
1. Lay the salmon fillets in a large, greased baking dish. Sprinkle lemon juice, pepper, dill, and garlic.
2. Prepare the oven at 400F, then place the dish and bake for about 20-25 minutes until the salmon is opaque.
3. Serve immediately.

Nutritional Info Per Serving:
Calories: 240, Fats: 14 g
Carbs: 0 g, Proteins: 28 g
Potassium: 228 mg, Sodium: 8 mg

Desserts

Cardamom Donuts

🍳 *Prep time: 10 minutes*

🍽 *Cook time: 18 minutes*

🍴 *Servings: 4*

Ingredients:
- 4 tbsp. almond flour
- 2 tbsp. flax meal
- 1 tsp. ground cardamom
- 2 tbsp. Erythritol
- 2 eggs, whisked
- 2 tbsp. unsweetened almond milk
- 1 tsp. coconut oil, melted

Directions:
1. In the mixing bowl, mix flax meal, almond flour, ground cardamom, whisked eggs, unsweetened almond milk, and melted coconut oil.
2. When the mixture is smooth, pour it into the donut cavities. Fill only 1/3 part of every donut cavity.
3. Bake the donuts in the oven at 350F for 18 minutes or until they are light brown.
4. Then remove the cooked donuts from the donut cavities and coat them with a mixture of Erythritol and cinnamon.
5. Do it very fast while donuts are hot.

Nutritional Info Per Serving:
Calories: 163, Fats: 12 g
Carbs: 7 g, Proteins: 7 g
Potassium: 134 mg, Sodium: 43 mg

Ginger Cookies

🍳 *Prep time: 15 minutes*

🍽 *Cook time: 8 minutes*

🍴 *Servings: 6*

Ingredients:
- 1 tsp. minced ginger
- ½ tsp. ground ginger
- ½ tsp. ground cinnamon
- 2 tbsp. Erythritol
- 1 tbsp. butter, softened
- ½ cup almond flour
- 3 tbsp. flax meal
- 2 tbsp. coconut oil

Directions:
1. Mix ground ginger, minced ginger, ground cinnamon, Erythritol, butter, flour, flax meal, and coconut oil.
2. Knead the dough and cut it into pieces.
3. Form balls from the dough.
4. Then press the center of every ball with the help of the tsp. to make the small holes.
5. Place the cookies in the tray and transfer them to the oven.
6. Bake the cookies at 360F for 8 minutes.

Nutritional Info Per Serving:
Calories: 74, Fats: 7.6 g
Carbs: 5 g, Proteins: 1.1 g
Potassium: 13 mg, Sodium: 18 mg

Coconut Pudding

Prep time: 10 minutes

Cook time: 9 minutes

Servings: 4

Ingredients:
- 1 2/3 cups light coconut milk
- 1/2 tsp. vanilla extract
- 3 egg yolks
- 1 tbsp. unflavored gelatin
- 6 tbsp. stevia

Directions:
1. In a bowl, mix gelatin with 1 tbsp. coconut milk; stir well and leave aside for now.
2. Put the rest of the milk into a pan and heat up over medium heat.
3. Add stevia; stir, and cook for 5 minutes
4. Mix hot coconut milk with the egg yolks and vanilla extract in a bowl; stir well and put the mixture to the pan.
5. Cook for 4 minutes, add gelatin and stir well.
6. Divide this into 4 ramekins and keep your pudding in the fridge until you serve it.

Nutritional Info Per Serving:
Calories: 92, Fats: 4 g
Carbs: 4 g, Proteins: 4 g
Potassium: 194 mg, Sodium: 10 mg

Sweet Zucchini Pie

Prep time: 15 minutes

Cook time: 50 minutes

Servings: 6

Ingredients:
- 1 zucchini, grated
- 2 eggs, whisked
- ½ tsp. baking powder
- 1 tbsp. Psyllium Husk
- ½ cup heavy cream
- 1 cup almond flour
- 2 tbsp. Erythritol
- ½ tsp. vanilla extract
- ¾ tsp. ground nutmeg
- 1 tsp. ground cinnamon

Directions:
1. Mix up together whisked eggs with heavy cream and Psyllium Husk.
2. Add baking powder, grated zucchini, almond flour, Erythritol, vanilla extract, ground nutmeg, and ground cinnamon.
3. Take the spoon and mix up the mass until homogenous.
4. Line the loaf pan with baking paper.
5. Pour the homogenous zucchini mass in the loaf pan, flatten it and cover with baking paper.

6. Bake the zucchini pie for 40 minutes at 350F.
7. Then remove the baking paper from the surface of the pie and bake it for 10 minutes more at 360F.
8. Chill the cooked pie very well and then cut into servings.

Nutritional Info Per Serving:
Calories: 105, Fats: 7.7 g
Carbs: 12.8 g, Proteins: 3.5 g
Potassium: 115 mg, Sodium: 38 mg

Kale Chips

Prep time: 10 minutes

Cook time: 15 minutes

Servings: 8

Ingredients:
- 1 bunch kale leaves
- 1 tbsp. olive oil
- 1 tsp. smoked paprika
- A pinch of black pepper

Directions:
1. Spread the kale leaves on a baking sheet, add black pepper, oil and paprika, toss, introduce in the oven and bake at 350 degrees F for 15 minutes.
2. Divide into bowls and serve as a snack.
3. Enjoy!

Nutritional Info Per Serving:
Calories: 177, Fats: 2 g
Carbs: 13 g, Proteins: 6 g
Potassium: 26 mg, Sodium: 1 mg

Chili Nuts with Ginger

Prep time: 10 minutes

Cook time: 10 minutes

Servings: 4

Ingredients:
- ½ tsp. chili flakes
- 1 egg white
- ½ tsp. curry powder
- ½ tsp. ginger powder
- 2 tbsp. honey
- A pinch of cayenne pepper
- 14 oz. unsalted mixed nuts

Directions:
1. In a bowl, whisk the egg white until foamy, add chili flakes, curry powder, ginger powder, honey, and cayenne pepper and whisk well.
2. Add the mixed nuts and toss well to coat.
3. Spread the nuts on a lined baking sheet and bake at 350 degrees F for 10 minutes, or until lightly golden.
4. Remove from oven and let cool.
5. Divide into bowls and serve as a snack.

Nutritional Info Per Serving:
Calories: 315, Fats: 22 g
Carbs: 22 g, Proteins: 10 g
Potassium: 348 mg, Sodium: 4 mg

Avocado and Chocolate Pudding

Prep time: 10 minutes
Cook time: 0 minutes
Servings: 2

Ingredients:
- 1 avocado, chunked
- 1 tbsp. natural sweetener such as stevia
- 2 oz. fat-free cream cheese, at room temp
- 1/4 tsp. vanilla extract
- 4 tbsp. cocoa powder, unsweetened

Directions:
1. Add all ingredients in a blender and blend until smooth.
2. Spoon in dessert bowls and chill for about 30 minutes and serve.

Nutritional Info Per Serving:
Calories: 215, Fats: 12 g
Carbs: 23 g, Proteins: 9 g
Potassium: 566mg, Sodium: 145 mg

Amazing Granola

Prep time: 15 minutes
Cook time: 30 minutes
Servings: 4

Ingredients:
- 1 cup coconut, unsweetened and shredded
- 1 cup almonds and pecans; chopped.
- 2 tbsp. coconut oil
- 1 tsp. nutmeg; ground
- 2 tbsp. stevia
- 1/2 cup pumpkin seeds
- 1/2 cup sunflower seeds
- 1 tsp. apple pie spice mix

Directions:
1. In a bowl, mix almonds and pecans with pumpkin seeds, sunflower seeds, coconut, nutmeg, and apple pie spice mix and stir well.
2. Heat a pan with the coconut oil over medium heat; add stevia and stir until they combine
3. Pour these over nuts and coconut mix and stir well.
4. Spread this on a lined baking sheet, introduce in the oven at 300 degrees F and bake for 30 minutes
5. Leave your granola to cool down, cut, and serve it.

Nutritional Info Per Serving:
Calories: 120, Fats: 2 g
Carbs: 4 g, Proteins: 7 g
Potassium: 485mg, Sodium: 103 mg

Banana Cake

Prep time: 10 minutes
Cook time: 25 minutes
Servings: 2

Ingredients:
- 2 cups whole wheat flour

- 1/4 cup cocoa powder
- 1 banana, peeled and mashed
- 1/2 tsp. baking soda
- 1/2 cup coconut sugar
- 3/4 cup almond milk
- 1/4 cup coconut oil, melted
- 1 egg
- 1 egg white
- 1 tsp. vanilla extract
- 1 tbsp. lemon juice
- Cooking spray

Directions:
1. In a bowl, combine baking soda, cocoa powder, flour, and sugar and stir.
2. Add banana, milk, oil, egg, egg white, vanilla, and lemon juice and stir well.
3. Grease a cake pan with cooking spray, pour the cake mix spread.
4. Bake at 350°F for 25 minutes, cool down, slice, and serve.

Nutritional Info Per Serving:
Calories: 270, Fats: 14 g
Carbs: 36 g, Proteins: 2 g
Potassium: 889mg, Sodium: 462mg

Matcha-Coconut Muffins

Prep time: 10 minutes

Cook time: 12 minutes

Servings: 4

Ingredients:
- ½ tsp. Matcha tea
- 2 tbsp. coconut flakes
- 1 cup coconut flour
- ½ tsp. baking powder
- ½ tsp. apple cider vinegar
- 1 tbsp. liquid stevia
- ¼ cup organic almond milk
- ½ tsp. ground ginger
- 1 tsp. butter, melted

Directions:
1. Put all ingredients in the big bowl.
2. Then use the hand mixer and blend the mixture until homogenous.
3. With the help of the spoon, put the blended mixture in the muffin molds.
4. Flatten the surface of the muffins if needed.
5. Let the muffins rest for 10 minutes.
6. Meanwhile, preheat the oven to 360F.
7. Transfer the muffins to the oven and cook them for 12 minutes.
8. When the muffins are cooked, remove them from the oven and chill for 5-10 minutes.
9. After this, remove them from the muffin molds.

Nutritional Info Per Serving:
Calories: 44, Fats: 3.1 g
Carbs: 3.5 g, Proteins: 0.9 g
Potassium: 248 mg, Sodium: 90 mg

Apple Cupcakes

Prep time: 10 minutes

Cook time: 20 minutes

Servings: 4

Ingredients:
- 4 tbsp. unsweetened applesauce
- 4 eggs
- 1 tsp. vanilla extract
- 3/4 cup almond flour
- 2 tsp. cinnamon powder
- 1/2 tsp. baking powder
- 1 apple, cored and sliced

Directions:
1. In a mixing bowl, combine applesauce, vanilla, and eggs.
2. Add almond flour, baking powder, and cinnamon, stir until well combined.
3. Divide the mixture into a lined cupcake pan.
4. Introduce in the oven at 350 degrees F and bake for 20 minutes.
5. Remove from the oven and let cool.
6. Top each cupcake with apple slices and serve.

Nutritional Info Per Serving:
Calories: 160, Fats: 9 g
Carbs: 13 g, Proteins: 7 g
Potassium: 210 mg, Sodium: 90 mg

Lemony Chickpea Dip

Prep time: 10 minutes

Cook time: 0 minutes

Servings: 4

Ingredients:
- 14 oz. canned chickpeas, drained, no-salt-added, rinsed
- Zest of 1 lemon
- Juice of 1 lemon
- 1 tbsp. olive oil
- 4 tbsp. pine nuts
- ½ cup coriander, chopped

Directions:
1. In a blender, combine the chickpeas with lemon zest, lemon juice, coriander and oil, pulse well, divide into small bowls, sprinkle pine nuts on top and serve as a party dip.
2. Enjoy!

Nutritional Info Per Serving:
Calories: 200, Fats: 12 g
Carbs: 9 g, Proteins: 7 g
Potassium: 144mg, Sodium: 212 mg

Blueberry Almond Flour Muffins

Prep time: 10 minutes

Cook time: 20 minutes

Servings: 6

Ingredients:
- 1/3 cup unsalted butter, softened

- 1 tsp. vanilla extract
- 1/2 cup honey
- 1 cup almond flour
- 1 cup fresh blueberries
- 2 large eggs
- 1 tsp. baking powder
- 1/2 tsp. lemon juice

Directions:
1. In a mixing bowl, beat the softened butter, vanilla extract, and honey until well combined.
2. Add the almond flour, eggs, baking powder, and lemon juice, and stir until smooth.
3. Gently fold in the blueberries.
4. Divide the batter evenly into the muffin cups.
5. Preheat the oven to 350F.
6. Bake the muffins for 20 minutes, or until a toothpick inserted into the center comes out clean.
7. Let the muffins cool in the pan for 5 minutes, then transfer to a wire rack to cool completely.

Nutritional Info Per Serving:
Calories: 215, Fats: 15.6 g
Carbs: 14.8 g, Proteins: 6.1 g
Potassium: 112 mg, Sodium: 24 mg

Rhubarb Pie

Prep time: 10 minutes
Cook time: 45 minutes
Servings: 8

Ingredients:
- 1 cup all-purpose flour
- 1 cup whole wheat flour
- 1/2 cup pecans, chopped
- 1/2 cup low-fat butter, melted
- 1/4 cup coconut sugar
- 4 cups rhubarb, chopped
- 1 cup strawberries, sliced
- 8 oz. low-fat cream cheese
- 1/2 cup honey
- 1/2 tsp. cinnamon
- 1/4 tsp. nutmeg

Directions:
1. In a bowl, mix the flours, pecans, melted butter, and coconut sugar until the mixture is crumbly.
2. Press the mixture into a 9-inch pie pan and bake at 350 degrees F for 10 minutes.
3. In a pan, combine the rhubarb, strawberries, cream cheese, honey, cinnamon, and nutmeg. Cook over medium heat for 5-7 minutes, stirring occasionally, until the rhubarb is soft.
4. Pour the rhubarb mixture into the pie crust and bake for an additional 35 minutes, until the filling is set.
5. Let the pie cool before serving.

Nutritional Info Per Serving:
Calories: 246, Fats: 9 g
Carbs: 39 g, Proteins: 4 g
Potassium: 346 mg, Sodium: 111 mg

Elegant Cranberry Muffins

Prep time: 10 minutes

Cook time: 20 minutes

Servings: 8

Ingredients:
- 2 cups almond flour
- 2 tsp. baking soda
- 1/3 cup unsweetened applesauce
- 1 whole egg
- 3/4 cup unsweetened almond milk
- 1/2 cup Erythritol
- Zest of 1 orange
- 2 tsp. ground cinnamon
- 2 cup fresh cranberries

Directions:
1. Preheat your oven to 350 °F.
2. Line a muffin tin with paper muffin cups and set aside.
3. Whisk the almond flour and baking soda in a mixing bowl.
4. In a separate bowl, combine the applesauce, egg, almond milk, Erythritol, orange zest, and cinnamon until fully incorporated.
5. Add the dry ingredients to the wet ingredients and stir just until combined.
6. Gently fold in the cranberries.
7. Divide the batter evenly among the muffin cups.
8. Bake for 20 minutes or until a toothpick inserted in the center of a muffin comes out clean.
9. Allow the muffins to cool for 10 minutes before serving.

Nutritional Info Per Serving:
Calories: 189, Fats: 13 g
Carbs: 16 g, Proteins: 5 g
Potassium: 123mg, Sodium: 398 mg

Cocoa Mug Cake

Prep time: 5 minutes

Cook time: 2 minutes

Servings: 1

Ingredients:
- 4 tbsp. almond meal
- 1 tbsp. coconut flour
- 1 tbsp. unsalted butter
- 1 tsp. honey
- 1/4 tsp. vanilla extract
- 1/2 tsp. baking powder
- 1 tsp. cocoa powder; unsweetened
- 1 egg
- Fresh berries for topping

Directions:
1. Melt the butter in a mug in the microwave for 30 seconds.

2. Add cocoa powder, honey, egg, baking powder, vanilla, and coconut flour, and stir well.
3. Add almond meal and stir again.
4. Place in the microwave and cook for 2 minutes.
5. Remove the mug from the microwave and allow it to cool for a few minutes.
6. Top with fresh berries and serve.

Nutritional Info Per Serving:
Calories: 320, Fats: 24 g
Carbs: 15 g, Proteins: 11 g
Potassium: 241mg, Sodium: 108 mg

Mint Bars

Prep time: 15 minutes

Cook time: 30 minutes

Servings: 4

Ingredients:
- 1 tsp. dried mint
- 1 egg, whisked
- 1 tbsp. olive oil
- ½ tsp. peppermint extract
- ½ cup almond flour
- 1 tbsp. honey
- ¾ cup unsweetened almond milk
- Cooking spray

Directions:
1. Place whisked egg, olive oil, and unsweetened almond milk in the mixing bowl.
2. Blend the mixture until homogenous.
3. Then add peppermint extract, almond flour, honey, and dried mint.
4. Stir the mass until you get a smooth batter.
5. Spray the spring form pan with the cooking spray.
6. Pour the mint butter into the pan and flatten its surface with the spatula.
7. Preheat the oven to 360F.
8. Transfer the spring form pan to the oven and bake it for 30 minutes.
9. Then switch off the oven and let the dessert rest for 10 minutes.
10. Remove the pan with dessert from the oven, cut it into bars, and transfer it to the serving plate.

Nutritional Info Per Serving:
Calories: 130, Fats: 9 g
Carbs: 8 g, Proteins: 3 g
Potassium: 82 mg, Sodium: 28 mg

Protein Bars

Prep time: 10 minutes

Cook time: 0 minutes

Servings: 4

Ingredients:
- 4 oz. apricots, dried
- 2 oz. water

- 2 tbsp. rolled oats
- 1 tbsp. sunflower seeds
- 2 tbsp. coconut, shredded
- 1 tbsp. sesame seeds
- 1 tbsp. cranberries
- 3 tbsp. hemp seeds
- 1 tbsp. chia seeds

Directions:
1. In your food processor, combine the apricots with the water and the oats, pulse well, transfer to a bowl, add coconut, sunflower seeds, sesame seeds, cranberries, hemp and chia seeds and stir until you obtain a paste.
2. Roll this into a log, wrap, cool in the fridge, slice and serve as a snack.
3. Enjoy!

Nutritional Info Per Serving:
Calories: 100, Fats: 3 g
Carbs: 8 g, Proteins: 5 g
Potassium: 140 mg, Sodium: 11 mg

Avocado Salsa

Prep time: 10 minutes

Cook time: 0 minutes

Servings: 4

Ingredients:
- 1 small yellow onion, minced
- 1 jalapeno, minced
- ¼ cup cilantro, chopped
- A pinch of black pepper
- 2 avocados, peeled, pitted, and cubed
- 2 tbsp. lime juice

Directions:
1. In a bowl, combine the onion with the jalapeno, cilantro, black pepper, avocado, and lime juice, toss and serve.
2. Enjoy!

Nutritional Info Per Serving:
Calories: 198, Fats: 2 g
Carbs: 14 g, Proteins: 7 g
Potassium: 540 mg, Sodium: 8 mg

Nut Cookies

Prep time: 15 minutes

Cook time: 10 minutes

Servings: 12

Ingredients:
- 2 tbsp. peanuts
- ¼ cup coconut milk
- 1 tsp. baking powder
- 1 cup almond flour
- ½ cup rice flour
- 2 tbsp. Erythritol
- ½ tsp. vanilla extract

Directions:
1. Chop the peanuts.
2. Mix up together coconut milk, baking powder, almond flour, and rice flour.
3. Stir gently and add Erythritol and vanilla extract.

4. Knead the dough.
5. Add peanuts and knead the dough again with the help of the hand palms.
6. Then cut the dough into 12 pieces.
7. Roll the small balls and press them gently with the help of a hand. The nut cookies are prepared.
8. Line the baking tray with parchment.
9. Put the nut cookies on the tray and transfer the tray in the preheated to the 360 F oven.
10. Bake the cookies for 10 minutes.
11. Remove the cooked cookies from the oven and chill them well.

Nutritional Info Per Serving:
Calories: 58, Fats: 3.2 g
Carbs: 6.6 g, Proteins: 1.3 g
Potassium: 95 mg, Sodium: 18 mg

Delicious Fruit Mousse

Prep time: 10 minutes

Cook time: 0 minutes

Servings: 12

Ingredients:
- 8 oz. low-fat cream cheese
- 1/2 pint blueberries
- 1/2 pint strawberries
- 1 cup low-fat whipped topping
- 3/4 tsp. vanilla extract
- 1 tsp. honey

Directions:
1. In a bowl, mix low-fat whipped topping, cream cheese, vanilla extract, and honey, and blend well using your mixer.
2. In each serving glass, layer blueberries, strawberries, and the cream cheese mixture, starting and ending with fruit.
3. Chill in the refrigerator for at least 1 hour before serving.

Nutritional Info Per Serving:
Calories: 92, Fats: 4 g
Carbs: 11 g, Proteins: 2 g
Potassium: 118 mg, Sodium: 77 mg

Easy Lemon Cream

Prep time: 10 minutes

Cook time: 15 minutes

Servings: 2

Ingredients:
- 3 cups unsweetened almond milk
- Juice of 2 lemons
- Lemon zest of 2 lemons, grated
- 2 tbsp honey
- 3 tbsp coconut oil
- 1 egg
- 2 tbsp gelatin
- 1 cup water

Directions:
1. In your blender, mix almond milk with lemon juice, lemon zest, honey, coconut oil, egg, and gelatin, and pulse well.
2. Divide the mixture into small jars and seal them.
3. Put the jars in a pan, add the water, place in the oven and cook at 380 degrees F for 15 minutes.
4. Serve the cream cold.

Nutritional Info Per Serving:
Calories: 98, Fats: 7 g
Carbs: 7 g, Proteins: 3 g
Potassium: 256 mg, Sodium: 62 mg

Vanilla Apple Mix

Prep time: 10 minutes

Cook time: 15 minutes

Servings: 2

Ingredients:
- 6 apples, cored and roughly chopped
- 4 tbsp. coconut sugar
- 2 tsp. vanilla extract
- 2 tsp. lemon juice
- 2 tsp. cinnamon powder

Directions:
1. In a small pan, combine the apples with the sugar, vanilla, lemon juice, and cinnamon, toss.
2. Heat up over medium heat, cook for about 10-15 minutes.
3. Divide between small dessert plates and serve.

Nutritional Info Per Serving:
Calories: 70, Fats: 0 g
Carbs: 16 g, Proteins: 1 g
Potassium: 607 mg, Sodium: 6 mg

Pumpkin Bars

Prep time: 15 minutes

Cook time: 15 minutes

Servings: 4

Ingredients:
- 1 tsp. pumpkin puree
- 1 egg, whisked
- ½ tsp. vanilla extract
- ½ cup almond flour
- ¼ tsp. ground cinnamon
- 1 tbsp. cream cheese
- ½ tsp. turmeric
- 1 tbsp. Erythritol

Directions:
1. Mix together pumpkin puree, whisked egg, vanilla extract, almond flour, ground cinnamon, cream cheese, turmeric, and Erythritol.
2. Transfer the smooth batter into the non-sticky square pan and flatten it with the help of a spatula.
3. After this, transfer the pan to the oven and bake it at 360F for 15 minutes.
4. The cooked pumpkin dessert will be soft and a little bit wet.

5. Chill the dessert for 10-15 minutes. Then cut it into the bars.

Nutritional Info Per Serving:
Calories: 48, Fats: 3.7 g
Carbs: 1.4 g, Proteins: 2.4 g
Potassium: 58 mg, Sodium: 44 mg

Baked Tortilla Chips with Chili

Prep time: 10 minutes
Cook time: 20 minutes
Servings: 6

Ingredients:
- 6 whole wheat tortillas, cut into 6 wedges each
- 1 tbsp. olive oil
- 1 tsp. chili powder
- 1/8 tsp. cayenne pepper
- 1/8 tsp. salt

Directions:
1. Preheat the oven to 350 degrees F.
2. Spread the tortilla wedges on a lined baking sheet and brush them with olive oil.
3. Sprinkle chili powder, cayenne pepper, and salt over the tortilla wedges.
4. Bake in the oven for about 10-12 minutes, flipping them halfway through, until they are crispy and light brown.
5. Remove from the oven and let them cool.
6. Serve as a side dish.
7. Enjoy!

Nutritional Info Per Serving:
Calories: 107, Fats: 3.3 g
Carbs: 16.5 g, Proteins: 3.3 g
Potassium: 98 mg, Sodium: 102 mg

Peanut Butter and Chia Pudding

Prep time: 10 minutes
Cook time: 0 minutes
Servings: 4

Ingredients:
- 1/4 cup peanut butter; unsweetened
- 2 cups almond milk; unsweetened
- 1 tsp. vanilla extract
- 1/2 cup chia seeds
- 1 tsp. vanilla stevia

Directions:
1. In a bowl, mix milk with chia seeds, peanut butter, vanilla extract, stevia and stir well.
2. Leave this pudding aside for 5 minutes, then stir it again, divide into dessert glasses and leave in the fridge for 10 minutes

Nutritional Info Per Serving:
Calories: 120, Fats: 1 g
Carbs: 4 g, Proteins: 2 g
Potassium: 135mg, Sodium: 326 mg

Blueberry Curd

Prep time: 10 minutes

Cook time: 10 minutes

Servings: 2

Ingredients:
- 2 tbsp. lemon juice
- 2 tbsp. coconut oil, melted
- 3 tbsp. honey
- 12 oz. blueberries
- 2 eggs

Directions:
1. Heat coconut oil in a pot over medium heat, add lemon juice and honey and whisk well.
2. Add the blueberries and eggs, whisk well, and cook for 10 minutes.
3. Divide into small cups and serve cold.

Nutritional Info Per Serving:
Calories: 188, Fats: 11 g
Carbs: 20 g, Proteins: 6 g
Potassium: 198mg, Sodium: 108 mg

Refreshing Watermelon Sorbet

Prep time: 20 minutes

Cook time: 0 minutes

Servings: 4

Ingredients:
- 2 cups watermelon, seedless and chunked
- ¼ cup of coconut sugar
- 2 tbsp. lime juice

Directions:
1. Add the listed fixing to a blender and puree. Freeze the mix for about 4- 6 hours until you have gelatin-like consistency.
2. Puree the mix once again in batches and return to the container. Chill overnight.
3. Allow the sorbet to stand for 5 minutes before serving and enjoy!

Nutritional Info Per Serving:
Calories: 91, Fats: 0 g
Carbs: 25 g, Proteins: 1 g
Potassium: 95 mg, Sodium: 1 mg

Dinner Recipes

Chinese-Style Beef Stir-fry

Prep time: 10 minutes

Cook time: 6 minutes

Servings: 2

Ingredients:
- 8 oz. beef sirloin, sliced into strips
- 2 tsp. canola oil
- ¾ cup orange juice
- 1 tsp. brown sugar
- 1 tbsp. apple cider vinegar
- 1 tsp. peanut oil
- 1 tbsp. soy sauce
- 2 tbsp. corn flour
- ¼ tsp. Chines 5-spice mix
- 1 tsp. chili flakes
- 3 cups mixed vegetables, cut stir fry style, frozen
- 2 tsp. minced fresh ginger
- 3 tsp. finely chopped garlic

Directions:
1. In a pan, fry the beef in 1 tsp. of hot oil for about 3-4 minutes, and set aside, covered to stay warm.
2. Make the sauce by combining the orange juice, sugar, vinegar, peanut oil, soy sauce, Chinese 5-spice, chili, and corn flour. Whisk well to incorporate the flour without any lumps.
3. Add the oil that remained to the wok and fry the garlic and ginger off for 1 minute. Add the veg mix and cook until thawed. Add in the sauce and cook for 2 minutes. Lastly, add the beef and cook until heated through and the sauce is thick and shiny.
4. Serve hot. Yum.

Nutritional Info Per Serving:

Calories: 321, Fats: 3 g
Carbs: 28 g, Proteins: 28g
Potassium:1278mg, Sodium:243 mg

Peppered Filet with Red wine sauce

Prep time: 7 minutes

Cook time: 6 minutes

Servings: 4

Ingredients:
- 1 cup low-sodium beef stock
- ¼ cup red wine
- ¼ cup finely chopped red onion
- ½ tsp. finely chopped rosemary, plus 4 sprigs to garnish
- 1 tbsp. unsalted butter
- 1 tsp. olive oil, plus extra in a spray bottle
- Black pepper to taste
- 4 6-oz. filet mignons
- 1 tsp. green peppercorns
- 1 tsp. red peppercorns
- ½ tsp. black peppercorn
- ½ tsp. white peppercorns

Directions:

1. First, make the sauce. Heat 1 tsp. of the oil in a small pot, add the onion and rosemary and fry off for about 2 minutes. Then add the wine and allow to reduce off almost completely.
2. Add the stock and simmer to reduce by half. Remove from the heat and whisk in the butter and black pepper to taste. Cover to keep warm.
3. Crush up all the peppercorns together. Place the filets on a plate and then crust them evenly on all sides with the peppercorns. Press the peppercorns into the meat to make sure it sticks.
4. Spray a non-stick pan with olive oil and heat. Cook the steaks at medium heat for about 4 minutes a side to get a medium-rare finish.
5. Serve hot with a tbsp. of the sauce drizzled over the tops and a sprig of rosemary to garnish.

Nutritional Info Per Serving:
Calories: 315, Fats: 14 g
Carbs: 2 g, Proteins: 34 g
Potassium: 833mg, Sodium: 132 mg

Chicken Tortilla Soup

Prep time: 10 minutes
Cook time: 18 minutes
Servings: 4

Ingredients:

- 1 tbsp. olive oil
- 1 onion, chopped
- 2 cloves of garlic, minced
- 2 tbsp. fresh cilantro, chopped
- 1 large ripe tomato, chopped
- 1 can black beans, drained and rinsed
- 1 cup frozen corn
- 4 cups chicken broth, low sodium
- 2 tsp. chili powder
- 1 tsp. cumin powder
- 1 bay leaf
- Pepper to taste
- 3 cooked chicken breasts, shredded
- 2 cooked corn tortillas, crumbled

Directions:

1. Place a pot on medium heat and heat for 3 minutes.
2. Add oil to the pot, stir to coat all parts of the pot.
3. Sauté the onion, tomato, and garlic for 5 minutes.
4. Stir in remaining ingredients except for tortillas.
5. Cover, bring to a boil, lower fire to a simmer, and simmer for 10 minutes.

6. Serve and enjoy with a sprinkle of crumbled tortillas.

Nutritional Info Per Serving:
Calories: 453, Fats: 10 g
Carbs: 40.1 g, Proteins: 19 g
Potassium: 991mg, Sodium: 935 mg

Spicy Enchilada Bake

Prep time: 15 minutes

Cook time: 35 minutes

Servings: 3

Ingredients:
- ½ tsp. olive oil, plus extra in a spray bottle
- 8 oz. lean ground turkey
- 1 small white onion, finely chopped
- 2 tsp. chili powder
- ¾ tsp. ground cumin
- ¼ tsp. ground paprika
- 4 tbsp. no-salt-added tomato paste
- 1 cup drained and rinsed black cooked beans
- ½ cup water
- 15 oz. cooked butternut squash, pureed
- ½ cup low-sodium chicken broth
- 4 whole wheat tortilla wraps
- 1/3 cup reduced-fat cheddar cheese, grated
- ½ cup nonfat plain Greek yogurt, to serve
- Sprig of parsley to garnish

Directions:
1. Sauté the onion in the olive oil in a medium skillet for 1 minute, then add the ground turkey and cook for about 8 minutes. Then add the chili powder, cumin, paprika, and tomato paste. Stir, add the black beans and water. Cook for about 2 minutes and set aside.
2. Preheat the oven to 350°F.
3. Next, make the sauce by heating up the butternut puree with the remaining spices and tomato paste. Then add the chicken broth and simmer on low until a smooth sauce is formed.
4. Oil a deep baking dish and then pour in ½ cup of the sauce and spread evenly over the bottom.
5. Divide the turkey mixture evenly amongst the wraps, then roll them up tightly and place snugly in the baking dish.
6. Cover the wraps evenly with the remaining sauce, add the grated cheese over the top and then bake for 20-25 minutes.
7. Serve with a spoonful of yogurt over the top, and a sprig of parsley to garnish.
8. Enjoy hot!

Nutritional Info Per Serving:
Calories: 440, Fats: 11 g
Carbs: 58 g, Proteins: 33 g
Potassium: 875mg, Sodium: 360mg

Dill Chicken Salad

Prep time: 15 minutes

Cook time: 10 minutes

Servings: 3

Ingredients:
- 1 tbsp. unsalted butter
- 1 small onion, diced
- 2 cloves garlic, minced
- 500g boneless skinless chicken breasts

Salad:
- 2/3 cup fat-free yogurt
- ¼ cup mayonnaise light
- 2 large shallots, minced
- ½ cup fresh dill, finely chopped

Directions:
1. Dissolve the butter over medium heat in a wide pan. Sauté onion and garlic in the butter and chicken breasts. Put water to cover the chicken breasts by 1 inch. Bring to a boil. Cover and reduce the heat to a bare simmer.
2. Cook for 10 minutes or until the chicken is cooked through. Cool thoroughly. Then shred chicken finely using 2 forks. Set aside. Whisk yogurt and mayonnaise. Then toss with the chicken. Add shallots and dill. Mix again all.
3. Serve and enjoy!

Nutritional Info Per Serving:
Calories: 253, Fats: 3.5g
Carbs: 9 g, Proteins: 3.1 g
Potassium: 679mg, Sodium: 278 mg

Cucumber and Seafood Bowl

Prep time: 15 minutes

Cook time: 12 minutes

Servings: 3

Ingredients:
- 2 cucumbers, chopped
- 1 tsp. mustard
- ½ tsp. ground coriander
- 1 tsp. margarine
- 6 oz. shrimps, peeled
- 4 oz. salmon, chopped
- 1 tbsp. low-fat yogurt

Directions:
1. Heat the margarine in the pan. Add the chopped salmon and cook for 2 minutes per side. Then add the shrimp and drizzle the coriander.
2. Close the lid and cook over low heat for 10 minutes. Then transfer them to serving bowls. Add the cucumbers. Mix the yogurt and mustard.
3. Sprinkle the food with the mustard mixture and serve.

Nutritional Info Per Serving:
Calories: 168, Fats: 5 g
Carbs: 9.5 g, Proteins: 22 g
Potassium: 367mg, Sodium: 682mg

Spicy Baked Sweet Potatoes

Prep time: 10 minutes

Cook time: 20 minutes

Servings: 2

Ingredients:
- 4 medium-sized sweet potatoes
- 1/2 cup black beans, canned, rinsed, and drained
- 1/2 cup Greek yogurt, non-fat
- 1 tsp. olive oil
- 1/2 tsp. taco seasoning, low-sodium
- 1/2 cup red pepper, diced
- 1/2 cup onion, chopped
- 1/2 tsp. paprika
- 1 tsp. chili powder
- 1/2 tsp. cumin
- 2 tbsp. shredded cheddar cheese, low-fat
- 1/2 cup salsa, low-sodium

Directions:
1. Preheat oven to 400°F (200°C).
2. Use a fork or another sharp kitchen tool to poke holes in the potato.
3. Bake the sweet potatoes for 45-50 minutes, until tender.
4. In a bowl, mix taco seasoning with Greek yogurt.
5. Heat oil in a saucepan at medium temperature.
6. Add chopped onions, paprika, chili powder, peppers, cumin, and sauté continuously on medium heat.
7. Wait for about 5 minutes to caramelize the onion.
8. Add the drained black beans; continue heating and stirring for about 5 minutes.
9. Using a fork, slice the sweet potatoes lengthwise.
10. Serve it by loading it with 2 tbsp. of shredded cheese, 2 tbsp. of Greek yogurt mixture, 1/4 of the black bean mixture, and 1/4 cup of salsa.

Nutritional Info Per Serving:
Calories: 296, Fats: 6 g
Carbs: 51 g, Proteins: 10 g
Potassium: 977mg, Sodium: 340 mg

Spicy Tomato Shrimp

Prep time: 15 minutes

Cook time: 8 minutes

Servings: 6

Ingredients:
- ¾ lb. shrimp, uncooked, peeled & deveined
- 2 tbsp. tomato paste (low-sodium)

- ½ tsp. garlic, minced
- ½ tsp. olive oil
- 1 ½ tsp. water
- ½ tsp. dried oregano
- ½ tsp. chipotle chili powder

Directions:
1. Rinse and dry the shrimp before setting them aside.
2. Get out a bowl and mix the tomato paste, water, chili powder, oil, oregano, and garlic. Spread this over the shrimp and make sure they're coated on both sides. Marinate for about 20 minutes or until you're ready to grill.
3. Preheat a gas grill to medium heat and then grease the grate with oil. Place it six inches from the heat source. Skewer the shrimp and grill for 2-3 minutes per side or until they are opaque.
4. Serve warm.

Nutritional Info Per Serving:
Calories: 88, Fats: 2g
Carbs: 5g, Proteins: 13g
Potassium: 158 mg, Sodium: 181 mg

Nutty Riced Vegetables

Prep time: 5 minutes
Cook time: 10 minutes
Servings: 4

Ingredients:
- 2 spring onions, finely chopped
- 3 tbsp. minced fresh garlic
- 1 tbsp. olive oil
- 2 cups riced cauliflower
- 2 cups riced sweet potato
- Black pepper to taste
- 2 tsp. fresh thyme, finely chopped
- ¼ cup cashews, roughly chopped
- ¼ cup fresh parsley, chopped

Directions:
1. Fry the spring onions and garlic in a medium pan in 1 tbsp. olive oil for about 4 minutes.
2. Add the cauliflower, sweet potato, and black pepper to taste, mix with a wooden spoon, and cook for 5-6 minutes.
3. Turn off the heat and then add in the thyme, cashews, and parsley.
4. Serve warm and enjoy.

Nutritional Info Per Serving:
Calories: 133, Fats: 10 g
Carbs: 10 g, Proteins: 4 g
Potassium: 428 mg, Sodium: 70 mg

Cream Dredged Corn Platter

Prep time: 10 minutes
Cook time: 4 hours
Servings: 3

Ingredients:
- 3 cups corn, fresh or frozen
- 2 oz. low-fat cream cheese, cubed
- 2 tbsp. low-fat milk
- 2 tbsp. low-fat whipping cream
- 2 tbsp. unsalted butter, melted
- Pepper as needed
- 1 tbsp. green onion, chopped

Directions:
1. Add corn, low-fat cream cheese, low-fat milk, low-fat whipping cream, unsalted butter, and pepper to your Slow Cooker.
2. Give it a nice toss to mix everything well.
3. Place the lid and cook on low for 4 hours.
4. Divide the mix amongst serving platters.
5. Sprinkle with chopped green onions.
6. Serve and enjoy!

Nutritional Info Per Serving:
Calories: 188, Fats: 7 g
Carbs: 27 g, Proteins: 7 g
Potassium: 465 mg, Sodium: 45 mg

White Bean Stew

Prep time: 15 minutes
Cook time: 55 minutes
Servings: 4

Ingredients:
- 1 cup white beans, soaked
- 1 cup vegetable broth
- 1 cup zucchini, chopped
- 1 tsp. tomato paste
- 1 tbsp. avocado oil
- 4 cups water
- ½ tsp. peppercorns
- ½ tsp. ground black pepper
- ¼ tsp. ground nutmeg

Directions:
1. Heat avocado oil in the saucepan, add zucchini, and roast them for 5 minutes. After this, add white beans, vegetable broth, tomato paste, water, peppercorns, ground black pepper, and ground nutmeg.
2. Simmer the stew for 50 minutes on low heat.

Nutritional Info Per Serving:
Calories: 184, Fats: 1 g
Carbs: 32.6 g, Proteins: 2.3 g
Potassium: 954mg, Sodium: 158 mg

Tasty Roasted Broccoli

Prep time: 5 minutes
Cook time: 20 minutes
Servings: 4

Ingredients:
- 4 cups broccoli florets
- 1 tbsp. olive oil
- Sunflower seeds and pepper to taste

Directions:
1. Preheat your oven to 400°F.
2. Add broccoli in a zip bag alongside oil and shake until coated.
3. Add seasoning and shake again.
4. Spread broccoli out on a baking sheet, bake for 20 minutes.
5. Let it cool and serve.
6. Enjoy!

Nutritional Info Per Serving:
Calories: 64, Fats: 4 g
Carbs: 4 g, Proteins: 4g
Potassium: 98 mg, Sodium: 14 mg

Pear Quesadillas

Prep time: 10 minutes

Cook time: 8 minutes

Servings: 2

Ingredients:
- 1 Cup pear, canned or fresh, cubed
- 1 cup cheddar cheese, grated
- 4 Medium size whole-wheat tortillas
- 1/2 cup green peppers, thinly chopped
- 2 Tbsp. Onion, finely chopped

Directions:
1. Place two tortillas on a cutting board.
2. Drizzle 1/4 of the shredded cheese on both tortillas.
3. Equally divide the peppers, pears, and onion and place on both tortillas. Now place the remaining cheese on both tortillas.
4. Top the tortillas with the remaining two tortillas.
5. Take a large non-stick sauté pan and bring it to medium heat. Place the tortillas in the pan.
6. Cook for about three minutes until the bottoms side becomes slightly brown.
7. Using a spatula, flip the tortilla and cook the other side for 3-4 minutes.
8. Once it is ready, gently transfer to a serving plate and cook the second tortillas.
9. Follow the same previous Directions and cook until it is ready.
10. Before serving, cut the tortillas into eatable sizes.
11. Serve hot, and you can refrigerate the balance for later consumption.

Nutritional Info Per Serving:
Calories: 217, Fats: 11 g
Carbs: 19 g, Proteins: 10 g
Potassium: 354mg, Sodium: 428mg

Parmesan Crusted Pork

🌿 *Prep time: 15 minutes*

🍳 *Cook time: 50 minutes*

🍽 *Servings: 3*

Ingredients:
- ¼ cup cornflakes, ground to breadcrumb size
- ¼ cup parmesan cheese, finely grated
- 1 tsp. fresh thyme, finely chopped
- 2 tsp. finely chopped garlic
- Black pepper to taste
- 16 oz. pork tenderloin
- Olive oil in a spray bottle
- 1 small red onion, sliced
- 4 sprigs fresh thyme to garnish

Directions:
1. Make your crumb mixture by mixing the cornflakes, parmesan, thyme, garlic, and black pepper in a shallow dish.
2. Roll the tenderloin in the crumbs, coating thickly and evenly on all sides.
3. Preheat the oven to 375°F.
4. Lightly oil a baking tray with olive oil, then lay the onion down on the tray. Place the crumbed tenderloin on top of the onions and bake in the oven for about 45-50 minutes.
5. Remove from the oven and then allow the tenderloin to rest for 10 minutes, covered.
6. Slice, and serve hot, garnished with a sprig of thyme.

Nutritional Info Per Serving:
Calories: 196, Fats: 6 g
Carbs: 28 g, Proteins: 1 g
Potassium: 746mg, Sodium: 243 mg

Cajun Chicken and Rice

🌿 *Prep time: 10 minutes*

🍳 *Cook time: 28 minutes*

🍽 *Servings: 5*

Ingredients:
- 1 tbsp. oil
- 1 onion, diced
- 3 cloves of garlic, minced
- 1 lb chicken breasts, sliced
- 1 tbsp. Cajun seasoning
- 1 tbsp. tomato paste
- 2 cups chicken broth, low sodium
- 1 ½ cups white rice, rinsed
- 1 bell pepper, chopped

Directions:
1. Place a pot on medium heat and heat for about two minutes.
2. Pour in the oil and stir to coat the pot with oil.
3. Sauté the onion and garlic until fragrant, around 3 minutes.

4. Stir in the chicken breasts and tomato paste. Season with Cajun seasoning. Sauté for 5 minutes.
5. Add broth and deglaze the pot. Stir in rice.
6. Cover, bring to a boil, lower heat to a simmer, and simmer for 5 minutes.
7. Stir in bell pepper. Continue simmering for another 10 minutes or until rice is absorbed.
8. Turn off the heat and let the rice sit for 5 minutes.
9. Serve and enjoy.

Nutritional Info Per Serving:
Calories: 389, Fats: 5.8g
Carbs: 50.4g, Proteins: 30.8g
Potassium: 487mg, Sodium: 584mg

Currant Pork Chops

Prep time: 15 minutes

Cook time: 7 minutes

Servings: 6

Ingredients:
- 2 tbsp. Dijon mustard
- 6 pork loin chops, center cut
- 2 tsp. olive oil
- 1/3 cup wine vinegar
- 1/4 cup black currant jam
- 6 orange slices
- 1/8 tsp. black pepper

Directions:
1. Start by mixing your mustard and jam together in a bowl.
2. Get out a non-stick skillet, and grease it with olive oil before placing it over medium heat. Cook your chops for 5 minutes per side, and then top with a tbsp. of the jam mixture. Cover, and allow it to cook for 2 minutes. Transfer them to a serving plate.
3. Pour your wine vinegar in the same skillet, and scape the bits up to deglaze the pan, mixing well. Drizzle this over your pork chops.
4. Garnish with pepper and orange slices before serving warm.

Nutritional Info Per Serving:
Calories: 265, Fats: 6 g
Carbs: 11 g, Proteins: 25 g
Potassium: 569mg, Sodium: 145 mg

Mac and Chokes

Prep time: 15 minutes

Cook time: 8 minutes

Servings: 6

Ingredients:
- 1 tbsp. olive oil
- 1 large diced onion
- 10 minced garlic cloves
- 1 can artichoke hearts, drained and rinsed
- 1 lb. whole wheat

- macaroni shells
- 12 oz. baby spinach
- 4 cups low-sodium vegetable broth
- 1 tsp. red pepper flakes
- 4 oz. reduced-fat vegan cheese
- ¼ cup cashew cream

Directions:
1. Set the pot to Sauté mode and add oil, allow the oil to heat up and add onions.
2. Cook for 2 minutes.
3. Add garlic and stir well.
4. Add artichoke hearts and sauté for 1 minute more.
5. Add uncooked pasta and 3 cups of broth alongside 2 cups of water.
6. Mix well.
7. Lock the lid and cook for 3 minutes on high pressure.
8. Quick release the pressure.
9. Open the pot and stir.
10. Add extra water, fold in spinach and cook in Sauté mode for 2 minutes.
11. Add cashew cream and grated vegan cheese.
12. Add pepper flakes and mix well.
13. Enjoy!

Nutritional Info Per Serving:
Calories: 360, Fats: 10 g
Carbs: 55 g, Proteins: 15 g
Potassium: 685mg, Sodium: 300mg

Chicken and Mushroom Stew

Prep time: 10 minutes
Cook time: 30 minutes
Servings: 4

Ingredients:
- 4 chicken breast halves, cut into bite-sized pieces
- 1-pound mushrooms, sliced
- 1 bunch spring onion, chopped
- 4 tbsp. olive oil
- 1 tsp. thyme
- Sunflower seeds and pepper as needed

Directions:
1. Take a large deep frying pan and place it over medium-high heat.
2. Add oil and let it heat up.
3. Add chicken and cook for 4-5 minutes per side until lightly browned.
4. Add spring onions and mushrooms, season with sunflower seeds, thyme and pepper according to your taste and stir.
5. Cover with lid and bring the mix to a boil.
6. Reduce heat and simmer for 25 minutes.
7. Serve!

Nutritional Info Per Serving:
Calories: 247, Fats: 12 g
Carbs: 10 g, Proteins: 23 g
Potassium: 1451mg, Sodium: 16 mg

Ethiopian Cabbage Delight

Prep time: 15 minutes

Cook time: 6-7 hours

Servings: 6

Ingredients:
- ½ cup water
- 1 head of green cabbage, cored and chopped
- 1 lb sweet potatoes, peeled and chopped
- 3 carrots, peeled and chopped
- 1 onion, sliced
- 1 tsp. extra-virgin olive oil
- ½ tsp. ground turmeric
- ½ tsp. ground cumin
- ¼ tsp. ground ginger

Directions:
1. Add water to your slow cooker.
2. Take a medium bowl and add cabbage, carrots, sweet potatoes, onion, and mix.
3. Add olive oil, turmeric, ginger, and cumin; toss until the veggies are fully coated.
4. Transfer veggie mix to your slow cooker.
5. Cover and cook on low for 6-7 hours. Serve and enjoy!

Nutritional Info Per Serving:
Calories: 155, Fats: 2 g
Carbs: 35 g, Proteins: 4 g
Potassium: 723 mg, Sodium: 58 mg

Healthy Mediterranean Lamb Chops

Prep time: 10 minutes

Cook time: 10 minutes

Servings: 4

Ingredients:
- 4 lamb shoulder chops, 8 oz. each
- 2 tbsp. Dijon mustard
- 2 tbsp. Balsamic vinegar
- ½ cup olive oil
- 2 tbsp. shredded fresh basil

Directions:
1. Pat your lamb chop dry using a kitchen towel and arrange them on a shallow glass baking dish.
2. Take a bowl and a whisk in Dijon mustard, balsamic vinegar, pepper and mix them well.
3. Whisk in the oil very slowly into the marinade until the mixture is smooth
4. Stir in basil.
5. Pour the marinade over the lamb chops and stir to coat both sides well.
6. Cover the chops and allow them to marinate for 1-4 hours (chilled).
7. Take the chops out and leave them for 30 minutes to allow the temperature to reach a normal level.

8. Preheat your grill to medium heat and add oil to the grate.
9. Grill the lamb chops for 5-10 minutes per side until both sides are browned.
10. Once the center reads 145°F, the chops are ready, serve and enjoy!

Nutritional Info Per Serving:
Calories: 521, Fats: 45 g
Carbs: 3.5 g, Proteins: 22 g
Potassium: 155 mg, Sodium: 149 mg

Walnuts and Asparagus Delight

Prep time: 5 minutes

Cook time: 5 minutes

Servings: 4

Ingredients:
- 1½ tbsp. olive oil
- ¾ pound asparagus, trimmed
- ¼ cup walnuts, chopped
- Sunflower seeds and pepper to taste

Directions:
1. Place a skillet over medium heat, add olive oil and let it heat up.
2. Add asparagus, sauté for 5 minutes until browned.
3. Season with sunflower seeds and pepper.
4. Remove heat.
5. Add walnuts and toss.
6. Serve warm!

Nutritional Info Per Serving:
Calories: 124, Fats: 12 g
Carbs: 2 g, Proteins: 3 g
Potassium: 307 mg, Sodium: 3 mg

Dash Diet Stewed Chicken Enchiladas

Prep time: 10 minutes

Cook time: 23 minutes

Servings: 6

Ingredients:
- 1 tbsp. olive oil
- 1 onion, chopped
- 3 cloves of garlic, minced
- 1.5 pounds chicken breasts, skinless
- 1 green bell pepper, chopped
- 1 can jalapeños, chopped (no added salt)
- 1 can diced tomatoes (no added salt)
- 1 can tomato sauce (no added salt)
- 1 tbsp. cumin
- 1 tbsp. chili powder
- 2 tsp. oregano, dried
- Pepper to taste

Directions:
1. Place a pot on medium-high and heat pot for three minutes.
2. Pour in olive oil and stir around to coat the pot with oil.
3. Sauté the onion and garlic until fragrant, around 3 minutes.

4. Add chicken breasts to the pot and cook until browned, around 5 minutes.
5. Add the green bell pepper, jalapeños, diced tomatoes, tomato sauce, cumin, chili powder, and oregano. Stir well.
6. As soon as the dish boils, cover the pan with a lid and simmer over low heat for 12 minutes until the chicken is fully cooked.
7. Take out the chicken breasts from the pan, shred the meat, and put it back into the pan. Mix it well with the other ingredients.
8. Preheat the oven to 350°F (180°C).
9. Scoop the chicken mixture into tortillas and roll them up. Place the enchiladas in a baking dish.
10. Bake for 8-10 minutes until the enchiladas are heated through.
11. Serve and enjoy.

Nutritional Info Per Serving:
Calories: 256, Fats: 8 g
Carbs: 15 g, Proteins: 30 g
Potassium: 676mg, Sodium: 209mg

Family Meatloaf

Prep time: 15 minutes
Cook time: 40 minutes
Servings: 8

Ingredients:
- ½ cup couscous
- 1 cup water
- 2 tbsp. finely chopped garlic
- 2 small bell peppers, diced
- 1 medium red onion, diced
- 1 tsp. mixed dried herbs
- 2 tbsp. olive oil, plus extra in a spray bottle
- ¼ cup plus 2 tbsp. barbeque sauce
- 1 tbsp. balsamic vinegar
- Black pepper to taste
- 2 large egg whites
- 17.5 oz. lean ground beef

Directions:
1. Place the couscous in a bowl. Bring the water to boil and pour it over the couscous. Cover, and leave to absorb the water for about 15-20 minutes.
2. Make your flavor base by heating olive oil in pan, then add the onion, paprika, garlic, and herbs and sauté for about 6 minutes. Set aside to cool.
3. Preheat the oven to 350°F.
4. Drain the couscous and then mix it in with the onion mixture. Add the barbeque sauce and balsamic vinegar and mix well. Season with black pepper to taste.
5. Mix in the egg whites, and finally stir in the raw ground beef.

6. Line a baking tray with foil, oil it, and shape the meat mixture into one medium-sized loaf. Bake for 40 minutes or until done.
7. Brush the last 2 tbsp. of barbeque sauce on top of the loaf in the last 5 minutes of cooking, and broil to caramelize.
8. Remove and let rest for 10 minutes.
9. Serve hot and sliced.

Nutritional Info Per Serving:
Calories: 162, Fats: 4 g
Carbs: 16 g, Proteins: 15 g
Potassium: 374mg, Sodium: 128 mg

Tuna Sandwich

Prep time: 5 minutes

Cook time: 0 minutes

Servings: 1

Ingredients:
- 2 slices whole-grain bread
- 1 6-oz. can low sodium tuna in water, in its juice
- 2 tsp. yogurt or low-fat mayonnaise
- 1 medium tomato, diced
- ½ small sweet onion, finely diced
- Lettuce leaves

Directions:
1. Toast whole grain bread slices. Mix tuna, yogurt, or mayonnaise, diced tomato, and onion. Cover the toasted bread with lettuce leaves and spread the tuna mixture on the sandwich.
2. Spread tuna mixed on toasted bread with lettuce leaves. Place another disc as a cover on top. Enjoy the sandwich.

Nutritional Info Per Serving:
Calories: 235, Fats: 3 g
Carbs: 25.9 g, Proteins: 27 g
Potassium: 891mg, Sodium: 395 mg

Elegant Pumpkin Chili Dish

Prep time: 10 minutes

Cook time: 25 minutes

Servings: 4

Ingredients:
- 3 cups yellow onion, chopped
- 8 garlic cloves, chopped
- 1 lb turkey, ground
- 2 cans (15 oz. each) fire-roasted tomatoes
- 2 cups pumpkin puree
- 1 cup chicken broth
- 4 tsp. chili spice
- 1 tsp. ground cinnamon
- 1 tsp. sea sunflower seeds

Directions:
1. Place a pot over medium heat.
2. Pour in coconut oil and heat it.

3. Add garlic and onion, sauté for four minutes.
4. Add the turkey and cook for 5 minutes.
5. Add in the remaining ingredients and bring the mix to simmer.
6. Simmer over low heat for 15 minutes.
7. Pour chicken broth.
8. Serve with desired salad.
9. Enjoy!

Nutritional Info Per Serving:
Calories: 312, Fats:16 g
Carbs: 14 g, Proteins: 27 g
Potassium: 1072mg, Sodium:644mg

Mediterranean Grilled Leg of Lamb

Prep time: 15 minutes

Cook time: 20 minutes

Servings: 6

Ingredients:
- 28-oz. leg of lamb, fat trimmed off, butterflied
- ½ cup unsweetened pomegranate juice
- ½ cup dry red wine
- 1 tsp. dried oregano
- 1 tsp. ground cumin
- 3 tbsp. finely chopped garlic
- ½ tsp. dried red pepper flakes
- Black pepper to taste
- ½ cup fresh pomegranate arils to garnish

Directions:
1. Place the lamb in a sealable container.
2. Mix together the pomegranate juice, red wine, oregano, cumin, garlic, and red pepper flakes to make the marinade. Pour the marinade over the lamb, ensuring that it fully covers the meat.
3. Refrigerate the lamb for at least 2 hours, stirring occasionally to ensure an even marinade. For best results, marinate overnight.
4. Preheat the grill to medium-high heat.
5. Peel the lamb from the marinade and season with black pepper to taste.
6. Oil a roasting rack and place the lamb on it. Place an oven tray underneath to catch the juices.
7. Grill the lamb for approximately 20 minutes, turning once halfway through, for a medium-rare leg of lamb.
8. Wait 5 minutes for the meat to rest, and cut it into portions. Put the lamb on a plate and garnish with fresh pomegranate seeds.
9. Serve hot and enjoy!

Nutritional Info Per Serving:
Calories: 258, Fats: 10g
Carbs: 7g, Proteins: 31g
Potassium: 510 mg, Sodium: 82 mg

Tasty Tortilla Bake

Prep time: 10 minutes

Cook time: 30 minutes

Servings: 2

Ingredients:
- 8 Tortilla, sliced into half
- 1 cup corn, frozen or fresh
- 1 onion, green, chopped
- 3 eggs
- 1 cup skim milk
- 1 cup reduced-fat Monterey Jack cheese
- 1 cup black beans, cooked
- 2 oz. green chilies, canned, chopped
- 1/2 tsp. chili powder
- 1 Tomato, sliced
- 1/4 cup salsa, no added salt or low-sodium

Directions:
1. Take an 8" square shaped baking tray and spray some cooking oil.
2. Set your oven to 370°F and preheat.
3. Layer in 5 tortilla halves in the bottom of the baking pan.
4. Top it with one-third of the cheese, beans, and corn layer by layer. Repeat the layering.
5. Beat egg in a bowl with chili powder, green chili, and skim milk. Now pour the mix over the tortilla.
6. Dress the tomato slice over the tortilla and spread the remaining cheese on top.
7. Bake it for 30 minutes and check to confirm its baking status.
8. Allow it to settle for another 10 minutes.
9. Serve with salsa.

Nutritional Info Per Serving:
Calories: 423, Fats: 14 g
Carbs: 52 g, Proteins: 23 g
Potassium: 897mg, Sodium: 488mg

Chicken Salsa

Prep time: 5 minutes

Cook time: 15 minutes

Servings: 2

Ingredients:
- 2 6-oz boneless, skinless chicken breasts
- 1 cup no-salt-added salsa
- 1 tbsp salt-free taco seasoning mix
- 1 cup non-fat plain Greek yogurt
- ½ cup low-sodium, reduced-fat cashew cheese, cubed

Directions:
1. Preheat a non-stick skillet over medium heat.

2. Add chicken breasts, 1/2 cup of salsa and taco seasoning. Mix well and cook for 12-15 minutes, until the chicken is cooked through.
3. Remove the chicken from the skillet and let it cool for a few minutes. Then cut it into cubes.
4. Place the chicken cubes on a toothpick and top each one with a cube of cashew cheese.
5. Serve with the remaining salsa and yogurt on the side for dipping.

Nutritional Info Per Serving:
Calories: 309, Fats: 7 g
Carbs: 20 g, Proteins: 42 g
Potassium: 778mg, Sodium: 436 mg

Turkey Wrap

Prep time: 15 minutes

Cook time: 0 minutes

Servings: 2

Ingredients:
- 2 slices of low-fat Turkey breast
- 4 tbsp. nonfat cream cheese
- ½ cup lettuce leaves
- ½ cup carrots, cut into sticks
- 2 homemade wraps or store-bought whole wheat tortilla wrap

Directions:
1. Prepare all the ingredients. Spread 2 tbsp. of nonfat cream cheese on each wrap. Arrange lettuce leaves, then add a slice of turkey breast; a slice of carrots stick on top. Roll and cut into half.
2. Serve and enjoy!

Nutritional Info Per Serving:
Calories: 224, Fats: 3.8 g
Carbs: 35 g, Proteins: 0.3 g
Potassium: 1490mg, Sodium:766mg

Tuscan White Beans with Shrimp, Spinach, and Feta

Prep time: 10 minutes

Cook time: 10 minutes

Servings: 5

Ingredients:
- 1 lb. shrimp, large, peeled, and deveined
- 10 oz. cannellini beans, saltless, rinsed, and drained
- 1 1/2 oz. low-fat feta cheese, shredded
- 1/2 cup chicken broth, fat-free, low-sodium
- 4 cloves clove Garlic, minced
- 2 tsp. sage, fresh, finely chopped
- 2 tbsp. balsamic vinegar
- 2 tbsp. olive oil
- 1 medium-size onion, chopped
- 5 cups baby spinach

Directions:
1. Take a large skillet
2. Pour in one tbsp. of olive oil and bring to medium temperature.
3. When the oil is hot, add the shrimp for 2-3 minutes.
4. Transfer the shrimp to a plate once its color changes.
5. Pour the olive oil into the skillet and put chopped onion, sage, and garlic.
6. Stir and cook until the onion turns a golden color. Within 4 minutes of cooking, the onion will start to become a golden color.
7. Add vinegar and continue cooking for another half minute.
8. Now add the chicken broth and cook for 2 minutes until it boils.
9. At this time, add the vegetables and spinach. Cook until the spinach starts to wilt.
10. Remove the skillet from the heat, add the cooked shrimp and stir.
11. Serve by topping with feta cheese.

Nutritional Info Per Serving:
Calories: 280, Fats: 7 g
Carbs: 22 g, Proteins: 32 g
Potassium: 814mg, Sodium: 756 mg

Sweet & Sour Pork Chops

Prep time: 10 minutes

Cook time: 1 hour 7 minutes

Servings: 4

Ingredients:
Sweet and Sour Cabbage:
- 1 tbsp. olive oil
- 1 medium red onion, sliced
- 2 slices of low-sodium turkey bacon, cut into cubes
- ½ medium-sized head of white cabbage, sliced
- ¼ cup apple cider vinegar
- 3 tbsp. honey
- ¼ cup low-sodium chicken broth
- 2 crisp green apples, peeled and diced
- Black pepper to taste

Pork Chops:
- Olive oil in a spray bottle
- 4 4oz. boneless pork chops, fat removed
- Black pepper to taste

Directions:
1. Heat oil in a pan and add sliced onions. Fry for 1 minute before adding bacon pieces. Cook until the bacon is crispy and browned. Add 1/3 of the cabbage and sprinkle over 1/3 of the vinegar. Repeat until all the cabbage and vinegar are incorporated.

2. Add honey, chicken broth, apples, and black pepper. Reduce heat and simmer for approximately 1 hour.
3. 10 minutes before the cabbage is ready, heat and oil a non-stick pan.
4. Fry pork chops until golden brown on each side, about 3 minutes per side. Season with black pepper and set aside, covered, to keep warm.
5. Transfer the cabbage mixture to the hot chops pan and stir well on high for 3 minutes.
6. To serve, use a slotted spoon to avoid getting juices on the plate. Spoon the cabbage mixture neatly onto the center of the plate and place the hot chops on top.
7. Enjoy!

Nutritional Info Per Serving:
Calories: 312, Fats: 9 g
Carbs: 38 g, Proteins: 26 g
Potassium: 778mg, Sodium: 136 mg

Middle American Pork and Beans

Prep time: 20 minutes

Cook time: 23 minutes

Servings: 4

Ingredients:
- 16-oz. pork tenderloin

Marinade
- 1 tsp. chili flakes
- 1 tsp. dried basil
- 1 tsp. dried cumin
- ½ tsp. paprika
- ¼ cup grapefruit juice
- 1 lime, zested and juiced
- 2 tbsp. olive oil

Beans
- 1 tbsp. canola oil
- 1 tbsp. ground cumin
- 2 tsp. dried basil
- 2 spring onions, finely chopped
- 2 small fresh paprika peppers
- 1 large ox heart tomato, diced
- 15 oz. cooked red kidney beans, drained
- ¼ cup chopped fresh parsley
- 2 tbsp. finely chopped fresh coriander

Directions:
1. Make the marinade first by incorporating all the marinade ingredients, except 1 tbsp. oil, together in a deep Tupperware dish. Place the pork in the Tupperware, making sure the marinade covers the top. Cover with the Tupperware lid.
2. Marinade the pork in the refrigerator for up to 1 hour.
3. To make the beans, heat the oil in a medium pan. Add the spring onions and

dried spices, and herbs and fry for about 2 minutes. Add paprika and cook for 4 more minutes, until the veg is soft. Then add the tomatoes, beans, and stock.
4. Reduce the heat on the beans and cover the pot, allowing it to simmer for approximately 5 minutes. During the last minute, add the parsley to the pot.
5. In the meantime, cook the pork tenderloin. Remove the pork from the marinade, but do not discard the marinade. Slice the pork into thin discs.
6. In a non-stick pan over medium heat, heat the remaining 1 tbsp. oil. Add the pork and fry for about 5 minutes or until fully cooked. Flip the pork over, pour the marinade into the pan, and cook for an additional 2 minutes.
7. Plate the beans and arrange the pork over the top attractively. Garnish with the chopped herbs and serve hot.

Nutritional Info Per Serving:
Calories: 319, Fats: 15 g
Carbs: 25 g, Proteins: 26 g
Potassium: 671mg, Sodium: 203 mg

Chickpea Cauliflower Tikka Masala

Prep time: 20 minutes

Cook time: 21 minutes

Servings: 6

Ingredients:
- 2 tbsp. olive oil
- 1 yellow onion, peeled and diced
- 4 garlic cloves, peeled and minced
- 1-inch piece fresh ginger, peeled and minced
- 2 tbsp. garam masala
- ½ tsp. ground black pepper
- ¼ tsp. ground cayenne pepper
- ½ small head cauliflower, small florets
- 2 15-oz cans chickpeas, rinsed and drained
- 1 15-oz can diced tomatoes, drained
- 1½ cups unsalted vegetable broth
- ½ 15-oz can coconut milk
- Zest and juice of 1 lime
- ½ cup fresh cilantro leaves, chopped, divided
- 1½ cups cooked fluffy brown rice, divided

Directions:

1. Warm up olive oil over medium heat, then put the onion and sauté for 4 to 5 minutes in a large Dutch oven or stockpot. Stir in the garlic, ginger, garam masala, black pepper, and cayenne pepper and toast for 30 to 60 seconds, until fragrant.
2. Stir in the cauliflower florets, chickpeas, diced tomatoes, and vegetable broth and increase to medium-high. Simmer for about fifteen minutes, until the cauliflower is fork-tender.
3. Remove, then stir in the coconut milk, lime juice, lime zest, and half of the cilantro. Taste and adjust the seasoning, if necessary.
4. Serve over the rice and the remaining chopped cilantro.

Nutritional Info Per Serving:

Calories: 323, Fats: 12 g
Carbs: 47g, Proteins: 11 g
Potassium: 516mg, Sodium: 444 mg

Chicken and Jasmine Rice

Prep time: 10 minutes
Cook time: 22 minutes
Servings: 6

Ingredients:

- 1 tbsp. olive oil
- 3 small shallots, diced
- 2 cloves of garlic, minced
- 1 lb. boneless, skinless chicken thighs, sliced thinly
- Pepper to taste
- 3 carrots, diced
- 1 ½ cups white jasmine rice, rinsed and drained
- 2 cups low sodium chicken broth
- 2 tbsp. thyme leaves

Directions:

1. Place a pot on medium heat.
2. Pour in the oil and stir to coat the pot.
3. Sauté the shallots and garlic until fragrant, around 3 minutes.
4. Stir in the chicken breasts and thyme leaves. Season with pepper. Sauté for 5 minutes.
5. Add broth and deglaze the pot. Stir in rice and carrots.
6. Cover, bring to a boil, lower heat to a simmer, and simmer for 12 minutes.
7. Turn off the heat and let the rice sit for 5 minutes.
8. Fluff rice, serve and enjoy.

Nutritional Info Per Serving:

Calories: 213, Fats: 7.9 g
Carbs: 27.1 g, Proteins: 10.1 g
Potassium: 366mg, Sodium: 324mg

Healthy Pork Fajitas

🍴 *Prep time: 10 minutes*

🍲 *Cook time: 15 minutes*

🍽 *Servings: 4*

Ingredients:
- 16 oz. pork loin, cut into slices
- 1 tbsp. olive oil
- 2 spring onions, cut into semi-thick slices at an angle
- 5 fresh paprika peppers sliced
- 2 tbsp. garlic finely chopped
- 1 tsp. smoked paprika
- 1 tsp. cumin
- ½ minced fresh chili
- Black pepper to taste
- 4 whole wheat flour wraps
- 1 avocado, peeled and cut into slices
- 1 lemon, cut into quarters
- Fresh coriander to serve

Directions:
1. Heat oil in a medium pan and fry the pork until well browned and fully cooked for about 5-10 minutes.
2. Set the pork aside.
3. In the same pan, add the spring onions, paprika, garlic, chili, dried spices, and black pepper. Fry for approximately 5 minutes until the vegetables are cooked. Then, return the pork to the pan and fry for an additional minute.
4. Heat a non-stick pan and lightly toast the wraps one by one.
5. Spoon the pork mixture into the wraps, add avocado fanned out on top, squeeze lemon juice, and garnish with fresh coriander.

Nutritional Info Per Serving:
Calories: 349, Fats: 12 g
Saturated fat: 2 g, Carbs: 36 g
Fiber: 7 g, Proteins: 27 g
Potassium: 1049mg, Sodium: 185mg

Zucchini Beef Sauté with Coriander Greens

🍴 *Prep time: 10 minutes*

🍲 *Cook time: 10 minutes*

🍽 *Servings: 4*

Ingredients:
- 10 oz. of beef, sliced into 1-2 inch strips
- 1 zucchini, cut into 2-inch strips
- ¼ cup cilantro, chopped
- 3 garlic cloves, minced
- 2 tbsp. reduced-sodium soy sauce
- 1 tbsp. olive oil

Directions:
1. Heat olive oil in a frying pan over high heat.
2. Add beef strips and brown for 5 minutes on high heat.

3. Once the meat is brown, add zucchini strips and sauté until tender.
   4. Once tender, add reduced-sodium soy sauce, garlic, and cilantro, and let them sit for 5 more minutes.
   5. Serve immediately and enjoy!

Nutritional Info Per Serving:
Calories: 245, Fats: 13 g
Carbs: 6 g, Proteins: 25 g
Potassium: 405mg, Sodium: 232mg

Beef Stir Fry

Prep time: 20 minutes

Cook time: 11 minutes

Servings: 4

Ingredients:
- 1 head broccoli chopped into florets
- 1 red bell pepper, sliced thin
- 1½ cups brown rice
- 2 scallions, sliced thin
- 2 tbsp. sesame seeds
- ¼ tsp. black pepper
- 1 lb. flank steak, sliced thin
- 2 tbsp. canola oil
- ¾ cup stir fry sauce

Directions:
1. Start by heating the oil in a large wok over medium-high heat. Add in your steak, seasoning with pepper. Cook for 4 minutes or until crisp. Remove it from the skillet.
2. Place your broccoli in the skillet and cook for 4 minutes. Toss occasionally. It should be tender but crisp.
3. Put your steak back in the skillet, and pour in your sauce. Allow it to simmer for 3 minutes.
4. Serve over rice with sesame seeds and scallions.

Nutritional Info Per Serving:
Calories: 408, Fats: 18 g
Carbs: 36 g, Proteins: 31 g
Potassium: 560 mg, Sodium: 171 mg

Chili-Lime Grilled Pineapple

Prep time: 5 minutes

Cook time: 4 minutes

Servings: 2

Ingredients:
- 1 fresh pineapple
- 2 tbsp. brown sugar
- 2 tbsp. lime juice
- 1 tbsp. olive oil
- 1 tbsp. honey or agave nectar
- 1-1/2 tsp. chili powder
- Dash of salt

Directions:
1. Peel pineapple, removing any eyes from the fruit.

2. Cut lengthwise into wedges; remove the core. In a small bowl, combine the remaining ingredients until they are blended.
3. Brush pineapple with half the glaze; reserve the remaining mixture for basting.
4. Grill pineapple for 2-4 minutes on each side or until lightly browned, occasionally basting with reserved glaze.

Nutritional Info Per Serving:
Calories: 97, Fats: 2 g
Carbs: 20 g, Proteins: 1 g
Potassium: 43 mg, Sodium: 107 mg

Italian Stuffed Portobello Mushroom Burgers

Prep time: 15 minutes

Cook time: 20 minutes

Servings: 4

Ingredients:
- 1 tbsp. olive oil
- 4 large Portobello mushrooms, washed and dried
- ½ yellow onion, peeled and diced
- 4 garlic cloves, peeled and minced
- 1 can cannellini beans, drained
- ½ cup fresh basil leaves, torn
- ½ cup panko bread crumbs
- ¼ tsp. ground black pepper
- 1 cup lower-sodium marinara, divided
- ½ cup shredded mozzarella cheese
- 4 whole-wheat buns, toasted
- 1 cup fresh arugula

Directions:
1. Heat up the olive oil in a large skillet to medium-high heat. Sear the mushrooms for 4 to 5 minutes per side, until slightly soft. Place on a baking sheet. Preheat the oven to a low broil.
2. Put the onion in the skillet and cook for 4 to 5 minutes, until slightly soft. Mix in the garlic then cook for 30 to 60 seconds. Move the onions plus garlic to a bowl.
3. Add the cannellini beans and smash with the back of a fork to form a chunky paste. Stir in the basil, bread crumbs, and black pepper and half of the marinara. Cook for 5 minutes.
4. Remove the bean mixture from the stove and divide among the mushroom caps. Spoon the remaining marinara over the stuffed mushrooms and top each

with the mozzarella cheese. Broil for 3 to 4 minutes, until the cheese is melted and bubbly.
5. Transfer the burgers to the toasted whole wheat buns and top with the arugula.

Nutritional Info Per Serving:
Calories: 407, Fats: 9 g
Carbs: 63 g, Proteins: 25 g
Potassium: 149mg, Sodium: 134 mg

Chicken and Vegetable Rice Pilaf

Prep time: 10 minutes

Cook time: 20 minutes

Servings: 6

Ingredients:
- 2 cups uncooked brown rice, rinsed
- 2 ½ cups low-sodium chicken stock
- 1 tbsp. olive oil
- 1 cup cooked chicken breast, shredded
- 2 small sweet potatoes, peeled and diced
- 2 carrots, diced
- 1 lb white mushrooms, sliced
- 1 lb green beans, trimmed and halved
- 3 cups kale, chopped
- 2 tbsp. low-sodium soy sauce
- 1 tbsp. rice vinegar

Directions:
1. Heat olive oil in a large saucepan.
2. Add the sweet potatoes and carrots, and sauté for 5 minutes.
3. Add the mushrooms and green beans, and sauté for an additional 5 minutes.
4. Stir in the chicken and cook for another 2 minutes.
5. Add the rice, chicken stock, soy sauce, and rice vinegar, and bring to a boil.
6. Lower heat to a simmer, cover the pot, and cook for 15-20 minutes or until the water is absorbed and the rice is tender.
7. Stir in the chopped kale and let it rest for 5 minutes before serving.

Nutritional Info Per Serving:
Calories: 320, Fats: 4.4 g
Carbs: 54.2 g, Proteins: 16.5 g
Potassium:1035mg, Sodium:280mg

Lean Meatballs in Tomato Sauce

Prep time: 15 minutes

Cook time: 25 minutes

Servings: 3

Ingredients:
- 2 tbsp. olive oil, divided
- 1 small white onion, finely chopped

- 6 oz. lean ground beef
- 2 oz. lean ground chicken
- 1 large egg
- ½ cup whole wheat breadcrumbs
- 2 tbsp. low-fat milk
- 2 tbsp. fresh parsley, finely chopped
- 2 tbsp. finely chopped thyme
- Black pepper to taste
- 1 tbsp. finely chopped garlic
- 1 14 oz. can no-salt-added chopped tomatoes
- ¼ tsp. chili flakes
- 3 oz. reduced-fat shredded cheddar cheese

▣ Directions:

1. Combine onion, ground beef, ground chicken, egg, breadcrumbs, milk, herbs, and black pepper in a mixing bowl. Roll the mixture into 9 meatballs.
2. Heat the olive oil (no more than 1 tablespoon) over medium heat in a deep, medium-sized skillet. Add the meatballs and cook for 6-7 minutes, turning occasionally to brown all sides. Transfer the meatballs to a plate.
3. Add the remaining olive oil to the same pan and sauté garlic and chili flakes for a minute before adding canned tomatoes. Cook for 2 minutes to reduce slightly.
4. Simmer the meatballs in a frying pan with tomato sauce over low heat for 10 minutes until the sauce thickens and the meatballs warm up.
5. While the meatballs are cooking, preheat the grill.
6. Sprinkle shredded cheese over the meatballs in the pan and place the pan under the grill for 2 minutes until the cheese melts and browns.
7. Garnish with chopped parsley and serve hot.

Nutritional Info Per Serving:
Calories: 413, Fats: 22 g
Carbs: 23 g, Proteins: 33 g
Potassium: 672 mg, Sodium: 203mg

Smoothies

Carrot-Cake Smoothie

Prep time: 5 minutes

Cook time: 0 minutes

Servings: 2

Ingredients:
- 1 frozen banana, peeled and diced
- 1 cup carrots, diced
- 1 cup nonfat or low-fat milk
- ½ cup nonfat or low-fat vanilla Greek yogurt
- ½ cup ice
- ¼ cup diced pineapple, frozen
- ½ tsp. ground cinnamon
- Pinch of nutmeg

Optional toppings:
- Chopped walnuts
- Grated carrots

Directions:
1. In a blender, combine the frozen banana, diced carrots, milk, Greek yogurt, ice, pineapple, cinnamon, and nutmeg.
2. Blend until smooth and creamy.
3. Pour the smoothie into glasses and serve immediately with optional toppings, if desired.

Nutritional Info Per Serving:
Calories: 180, Fats: 1 g
Carbs: 36 g, Proteins: 8 g
Potassium: 640mg, Sodium: 133 mg

Coconut Spiced Apple Smoothie

Prep time: 5 minutes

Cook time: 0 minutes

Servings: 2

Ingredients:
- 1 apple
- 2 tbsp. almond butter
- ¼ tsp. cinnamon powder
- 1 pinch ground ginger
- 2 tbsp. hemp seeds
- 2 tbsp. honey
- 1 cup coconut milk

Directions:
1. Start by preparing all the ingredients, then combine all the ingredients in your blender, then pulse until smooth and well blended.
2. Pour the smoothies in tall glasses.
3. Serve and enjoy!

Nutritional Info Per Serving:
Calories: 123, Fats: 14.6 g
Carbs: 8.6 g, Proteins: 4.6 g
Potassium: 602 mg, Sodium: 57 mg

Ginger Berry Smoothie

✂ *Prep time: 6 minutes*

🍲 *Cook time: 0 minutes*

🍽 *Servings: 1*

Ingredients:
- ½ cup unsweetened almond milk
- 1 cup mixed berries
- ½ cup unsweetened plain yogurt
- 1-piece fresh ginger, minced
- 4 or 5 ice cubes

Directions:
1. Combine all the ingredients in your blender, then pulse until smooth and well blended.
2. Serve and enjoy!

Nutritional Info Per Serving:
Calories: 146, Fats: 14 g
Carbs: 8 g, Proteins: 4 g
Potassium: 456mg, Sodium: 578 mg

Flaxseed & Banana Smoothie

✂ *Prep time: 5 minutes*

🍲 *Cook time: 0 minutes*

🍽 *Servings: 1*

Ingredients:
- 1 frozen banana
- 2 tbsp. ground flaxseed
- ½ cup unsweetened almond milk
- 1 tsp. vanilla extract
- 1 tsp. honey
- 1 tbsp. almond butter

Directions:
1. Mix all ingredients in a blender and pour the smoothie into a glass.
2. Enjoy!

Nutritional Info Per Serving:
Calories: 356, Fats: 18.3 g
Carbs: 45.1 g, Proteins: 8.4 g
Potassium: 527 mg, Sodium: 97 mg

Peanut Butter and Banana Smoothie

✂ *Prep time: 5 minutes*

🍲 *Cook time: 0 minutes*

🍽 *Servings: 1*

Ingredients:
- 1 cup nonfat or low-fat milk
- 1 cup ice
- ¼ cup plain nonfat or low-fat Greek yogurt
- 1 frozen banana, sliced
- 1 tbsp. peanut butter

Directions:
1. Mix the ingredients into a blender and process until smooth.
2. Enjoy immediately.

Nutritional Info Per Serving:
Calories: 313, Fats: 9 g
Carbs: 45 g, Proteins: 19 g
Potassium: 858mg, Sodium: 476mg

Pumpkin Spice Smoothie

Prep time: 5 minutes

Cook time: 0 minutes

Servings: 2

Ingredients:
- 1 cup unsweetened almond milk
- 1/2 tsp. pumpkin pie spice
- 1/4 tsp. ground cinnamon
- 1 small banana
- 3/4 cup fat-free plain Greek yogurt
- 1/2 cup canned pumpkin puree
- 1 tbsp. pure maple syrup
- 1 cup ice (about 10 cubes)

Directions:
1. Place all ingredients, except for the ice, in a blender and blend until smooth.
2. Depending on the desired thickness, continue adding ice until you reach the desired consistency.
3. Transfer the mixture into individual glasses and serve.

Nutritional Info Per Serving:
Calories: 140, Fats: 1.5 g
Carbs: 23 g, Proteins: 9 g
Potassium: 428 mg, Sodium: 87 mg

Peaches and Greens Smoothie

Prep time: 5 minutes

Cook time: 0 minutes

Servings: 1

Ingredients:
- 2 cups fresh spinach
- 1 cup frozen peaches or fresh, pitted
- 1 cup ice
- ½ cup nonfat or low-fat milk
- ½ cup plain nonfat Greek yogurt
- ½ tsp. vanilla extract

Optional:
- No-calorie sweetener choice

Directions:
1. Put all ingredients in a blender and blend thoroughly.
2. Serve and enjoy.

Nutritional Info Per Serving:
Calories: 191, Fats: 0 g
Carbs: 30 g, Proteins: 18 g
Potassium: 1131mg, Sodium: 190mg

Peanut Butter Banana Smoothie

Prep time: 5 minutes

Cook time: 0 minutes

Servings: 2

Ingredients:
- 1 banana
- 1/2 cup sliced cucumbers
- 1 tbsp. natural peanut butter
- 1/2 cup unsweetened almond milk
- 1/2 cup ice

Directions:
1. Mix all ingredients together in a blender.
2. Pour the smoothie into glasses and serve.

Nutritional Info Per Serving:
Calories: 119, Fats: 6 g
Carbs: 14 g, Proteins: 4 g
Potassium: 262 mg, Sodium: 87 mg

Strawberry Yogurt Smoothie

Prep time: 5 minutes

Cook time: 0 minutes

Servings: 1

Ingredients:
- 1 cup plain nonfat
- 1 cup frozen strawberries
- 1 cup ice
- ½ cup nonfat or low-fat milk
- ½ orange, peeled
- ½ frozen banana

Directions:
1. Put all ingredients in a blender and blend thoroughly.
2. Serve.

Nutritional Info Per Serving:
Calories: 305, Fats: 1 g
Carbs: 52 g, Proteins: 29 g
Potassium: 795mg, Sodium: 132 mg

Orange and Peach Smoothie

Prep time: 5 minutes

Cook time: 0 minutes

Servings: 2

Ingredients:
- 2 oranges, cut into segments
- 2 peaches, pitted and sliced
- 1 cup carrot juice
- ¼ tsp. cinnamon powder
- 1 pinch ground ginger
- 2 tbsp. ground flaxseeds
- 1 tbsp. chia seeds

Directions:
1. Combine all the ingredients in your blender, then pulse until smooth and well blended.
2. Pour the smoothies in tall glasses.
3. Serve and enjoy!

Nutritional Info Per Serving:
Calories: 115, Fats: 14.6 g
Carbs: 8.6 g, Proteins: 4.6 g
Potassium: 430 mg, Sodium: 81 mg

Banana-Peanut Butter 'n Greens Smoothie

Prep time: 7 minutes

Cook time: 0 minutes

Servings: 2

Ingredients:
- 1 cup chopped and packed Romaine lettuce
- 1 frozen medium banana
- 1 tbsp. natural peanut butter
- 1 cup unsweetened almond milk

Directions:
1. In a heavy-duty blender, add all ingredients.
2. Puree until smooth and creamy.
3. Serve and enjoy.

Nutritional Info Per Serving:
Calories: 183, Fats: 7 g
Carbs: 29 g, Proteins: 5 g
Potassium: 327mg, Sodium: 110 mg

Coco Strawberry Smoothie

Prep time: 4 minutes

Cook time: 0 minutes

Servings: 1

Ingredients:
- 1 cup frozen strawberries, washed and chopped
- 1 cup unsweetened coconut milk,
- 2 tbsp. almond butter
- 1 tbsp. peanut butter
- 2 packets stevia
- 1 tsp. chia seeds
- Crushed ice
- Mint leaves

Directions:
1. Add the strawberries to a blender, then stir in the almond butter, coconut milk, peanut butter, chia seeds, stevia drops and blend it using a hand blender.
2. Pour in a tall glass and add crushed ice.
3. Garnish with mint leaves and serve.
4. Enjoy!

Nutritional Info Per Serving:
Calories: 155, Fats: 9 g
Carbs: 8.6 g, Proteins: 5 g
Potassium: 609mg, Sodium: 318 mg

Fruity Tofu Smoothie

Prep time: 5 minutes

Cook time: 0 minutes

Servings: 2

Ingredients:
- 1 cup ice cold water
- 1 container silken tofu
- ¼ cup frozen mango chunks
- 1 frozen medium banana
- ½ cup frozen pineapple chunks
- 1 cup packed spinach
- 1 tbsp. chia seeds

Directions:
1. Put all ingredients in a blender and blend thoroughly.
2. Evenly divide into two glasses, serve and enjoy.

Nutritional Info Per Serving:
Calories: 175, Fats: 3.7 g
Carbs: 33.3 g, Proteins: 6.0 g
Potassium: 391 mg, Sodium: 16 mg

Orange Juice Smoothie

Prep time: 5 minutes

Cook time: 0 minutes

Servings: 2

Ingredients:
- 1/4 cup frozen orange juice concentrate
- 3/4 cup fat-free milk
- 1 cup fat-free vanilla frozen yogurt

Directions:
1. Add the ingredients to a blender and pulse until they're smooth.
2. Pour them into frosted glasses and serve.

Nutritional Info Per Serving:
Calories: 180, Fats: 0 g
Carbs: 38 g, Proteins: 7 g
Potassium: 525mg, Sodium: 124 mg

Cantaloupe Dash Smoothie

Prep time: 5 minutes

Cook time: 0 minutes

Servings: 2

Ingredients:
- 1/4 cups frozen cantaloupe
- ½ nonfat or low-fat milk
- 1 sliced, frozen banana
- 5 oz. nonfat vanilla Greek yogurt
- ½ cup ice
- 1 tsp. honey

Directions:
1. Peel, cube, and freeze the cantaloupe.
2. Place the milk, banana, yogurt, ice, and honey in a blender.
3. Work and mix the fixings till incorporated and creamy.
4. Toss in the cantaloupe pieces - process until incorporated and creamy smooth.
5. Serve immediately.

Nutritional Info Per Serving:
Calories: 214, Fats: 1 g
Carbs: 46 g, Proteins: 10 g
Potassium: 201 mg, Sodium: 55 mg

Creamy Blueberry Oat Smoothie

Prep time: 4 minutes

Cook time: 0 minutes

Servings: 1

Ingredients:
- 1 cup unsweetened almond milk
- 1 tbsp. ground flaxseed
- 1 cup baby spinach
- ½ cup fresh or frozen blueberries
- ½ cup cooked steel-cut oats, chilled

Directions:

1. Mix all ingredients in a blender and pour the smoothie into a glass.
2. Serve immediately.

Nutritional Info Per Serving:

Calories: 272, Fats: 8.3 g
Carbs: 38 g, Proteins: 12 g
Potassium: 400mg, Sodium: 145 mg

Conclusion

Congratulations! You have reached the end of this book and have gained valuable insights into the DASH Diet. I hope the information, personal experiences, and practical advice shared in this book have inspired you to take the first steps towards a healthier lifestyle with the DASH Diet.

As we have discussed, the DASH Diet is a science-based eating pattern that emphasizes whole grains, vegetables, fruits, lean proteins, and low-fat dairy products. It is intentionally designed to effectively lower blood pressure, minimize the risk of chronic disease, and promote optimal health and well-being. The DASH Diet is not a fad diet or a quick fix but rather a sustainable and balanced approach to eating that can benefit people of all ages and lifestyles.

Throughout this book, we have explored the benefits of the DASH Diet, including its impact on heart health, weight management, and overall health. We have discussed the scientific basis and principles of the DASH Diet, including its focus on nutrient-rich foods, portion sizes, and sodium reduction. We have also addressed common questions and concerns that readers may have, such as incorporating the DASH Diet into everyday life, making food choices, dining out, accommodating dietary restrictions, and more.

I want to reiterate some key concepts and highlights of the DASH Diet that are worth remembering as you embark on your own DASH Diet journey:

1. **Focus on nutrient-rich foods:** Opt for a well-rounded plate that includes a diverse selection of whole grains, lean proteins, vegetables, fruits, and low-fat dairy products to ensure obtaining a broad spectrum of essential nutrients for optimal health and well-being.

2. **Pay attention to portion sizes:** Be mindful of portion sizes to avoid overeating and promote weight management. Use smaller plates and bowls and pay close attention to your body's cues of hunger and fullness.

3. **Reduce sodium intake:** Limit your intake of sodium by choosing fresh or minimally processed foods, reading food labels, and cooking at home using herbs, spices, and other flavor-enhancing techniques.

4. **Make gradual changes:** Instead of trying to overhaul your entire diet at once, make small, sustainable changes over time to create lasting habits.

5. **Stay hydrated:** Ensure optimal health by drinking enough water throughout the day to support your body's needs.

6. **Seek support and guidance:** Consider enlisting the support of a registered dietitian or healthcare provider to create a customized meal plan and receive ongoing guidance and support as you follow the DASH Diet.

7. **Listen to your body:** Pay attention to how different foods make you feel and adjust your eating pattern accordingly. Recognize that everyone's nutritional needs and preferences are unique, and prioritize listening to your body and making choices that align with your individual needs when following the DASH Diet.

As you embark on your DASH Diet journey, remember that progress, not perfection, is the key. Practice self-compassion and celebrate even the smallest successes on your DASH Diet journey. Being kind to yourself and acknowledging your progress is important for maintaining motivation and building a positive relationship with food and health. Embrace the DASH Diet as a long-term lifestyle change and not a short-term fix.

With consistent effort and commitment, you can achieve improved health, well-being, and quality of life with the DASH Diet.

I wish you the best of luck on your DASH Diet journey! Remember, you can take control of your health and make positive changes through your food choices. Here's to a healthier and happier you with the DASH Diet!

Sincerely, Phyllis Fletcher

Measurement Conversion Chart

Volume Equivalents (Liquid)

US STANDARD	US STANDARD (OZ.)	METRIC (APPROXIMATE)
2 tbsp.	1 fl. oz.	30 mL
¼ cup	2 fl. oz.	60 mL
1/2 cup	4 fl. oz.	120 mL
1 cup	8 fl. oz.	240 mL
1 1/2 cups	12 fl. oz.	355 mL
2 cups or 1 pint	16 fl. oz.	475 mL
4 cups or 1 quart	32 fl. oz.	1 L
1 gallon	128 fl. oz.	4 L

Volume Equivalents (Dry)

US STANDARD	METRIC (APPROXIMATE)
¼ tsp.	1 mL
½ tsp.	2 mL
1 tsp.	5 mL
1 tbsp.	15 mL
¼ cup	59 mL
1/3 cup	79 mL
1/2 cup	118 mL
1 cup	177 mL

US STANDARD	METRIC (APPROXIMATE)
1/2 oz.	15 g
1 oz.	30 g
2 oz.	60 g
4 oz.	115 g
8 oz.	225 g
12 oz.	340 g
16 oz. or 1 pound	455 g

Index

A

Almond Butternut Chicken 77
Amazing Granola 86
Apple-Apricot Brown Rice Breakfast Porridge 39
Apple Blue Cheese Salad 53
Apple Cupcakes 88
Apple Oats 32
Aromatic Breakfast Granola 22
Aromatic Spaghetti 80
Artichoke Spinach Chicken 80
Arugula Salad 56
Asparagus Omelet 25
Avocado and Chocolate Pudding 86
Avocado and Egg Toast 22
Avocado Cup with Egg 36
Avocado Salsa 92
Avocado Sandwich with Lemon and Cilantro 63
Avocado, Tomato, and Olives Salad 46

B

Bagels Made Healthy 23
Baked Eggs in Avocado 79
Baked Tortilla Chips with Chili 95
Baked Whole Wheat Macaroni and Beef Casserole 76
Balsamic Cabbage 46
Balsamic Chicken and Vegetables 64
Banana Cake 86
Banana & Cinnamon Oatmeal 33
Banana-Peanut Butter 'n Greens Smoothie 127
Bean Frittata 26
Beef Pot Roast 74
Beef Stir Fry 120
Blueberry Almond Flour Muffins 88
Blueberry Curd 96
Blueberry Muffins 25
Blueberry-Oatmeal Muffin in a Mug 37
Blueberry Whole Wheat Waffles 24
Breakfast Splits 38
Buckwheat Crepes 27
Buffalo Chicken Lettuce Wraps 75
Butternut Squash Apple Salad 52

C

Cajun Chicken and Rice 105
Cantaloupe Dash Smoothie 129
Cardamom Donuts 83
Carrot Cake Overnight Oats 31
Carrot-Cake Smoothie 124
Cauliflower "Mac and Cheese" Casserole 59
Cereal with Cranberry Orange Twist 27
Chicken and Broccoli 68
Chicken and Jasmine Rice 118
Chicken and Mushroom Stew 107
Chicken and Vegetable Rice Pilaf 122
Chicken Salsa 113
Chicken Tortilla Soup 98
Chicken Vegetable Soup 66
Chickpea Cauliflower Tikka Masala 117
Chili Broccoli 43
Chili-Lime Grilled Pineapple 120

Chili Nuts with Ginger 85
Chinese-Style Beef Stir-fry 97
Chipotle Lettuce Chicken 81
Choco-Fudge Cookies 50
Cilantro Lime Rice 49
Cobb Salad 78
Cocoa Mug Cake 90
Coconut Crepes 38
Coconut Pudding 84
Coconut Spiced
Apple Smoothie 124
Coconut, Strawberries,
and Chocolate 45
Coco Strawberry Smoothie 128
Cream Dredged
Corn Platter 102
Creamy Blueberry
Oat Smoothie 129
Creamy Broccoli Cheddar Rice 41
Creamy Cauliflower Mash 56
Cucumber and
Seafood Bowl 100
Currant Pork Chops 106
Curried Chicken wrap 72
Curry Tofu Scramble 33

D

Danish Style Duck with Cucumber
and Carrots 60
Dash Apple Pancakes 29
Dash Diet Stewed
Chicken Enchiladas 109
Delicious Fruit Mousse 93
Dill Chicken Salad 100

E

Easy Lemon Cream 93
Easy Roasted Salmon 82
Easy Salmon Steaks 59
Egg Toasts 31
Elegant Cranberry Muffins 90
Elegant Pumpkin
Chili Dish 111
Ethiopian Cabbage Delight 108

F

Family Meatloaf 110
Flat Bread Pizza 65
Flaxseed & Banana Smoothie 125
French Toast with Applesauce 30
Fruits and Rice Pudding 23
Fruity Tofu Smoothie 128

G

Garlic Potato Pan 55
Ginger Berry Smoothie 125
Ginger Cookies 83
Greek Yogurt Oat Pancakes 35
Grilled Flank Steak
with Lime Vinaigrette 66

H

Healthy Avocado
Beef Patties 75
Healthy Mediterranean Lamb Chops 108
Healthy Pork Fajitas 119
Healthy Vegetable
Fried Rice 72

I

Instant Banana Oatmeal 29
Italian Roast Mushrooms 52
Italian Stuffed Portobello Mushroom
Burgers 121

J

Japanese Potato and
Beef Croquettes 62

K

Kale Chips 85

L

Lean Meatballs in
Tomato Sauce 122
Lemon Asparagus 41
Lemony Chickpea Dip 88
Lentil Avocado Tacos 61
Lime Carrots 49

M

Mac and Chokes 106
Matcha-Coconut Muffins 87
Mediterranean Grilled
Leg of Lamb 112
Mediterranean Shrimp Pasta with
    Artichokes and Spinach 79
Mediterranean Toast 28
Middle American
Pork and Beans 116
Mint Bars 91
Moist Chocolate Brownies 55

N

New York Strip Steak with
    Mushroom Sauce 68
No-Cook Overnight Oats 36
No-Mayo Potato Salad 43
Nut Cookies 92
Nutty Riced Vegetables 102

O

Oatmeal Banana Pancakes
with Walnuts 23
Open-Faced Garden
Tuna Sandwich 81
Orange and Peach Smoothie 127
Orange Juice Smoothie 129

P

Paella with Chicken,
Leeks, and Tarragon 63
Paprika Brussels sprouts 57
Parmesan Crusted Pork 105
Parmesan Endives 44
Peaches and
Greens Smoothie 126
Peach Pancakes 32
Peanut and Chocolate Squares 47
Peanut Butter and
Banana Smoothie 125
Peanut Butter and
Chia Pudding 95
Peanut Butter
Banana Smoothie 126
Pear Quesadillas 104
Peppered Filet with
Red wine sauce 97
Peppery Beef Tenderloin 70
Pork and Roasted
Tomato Mix 71
Protein Bars 91
Pumpkin Bars 94
Pumpkin Spice Smoothie 126

Q

Quinoa Bowl 39

R

Raspberry Yogurt 28
Red Beans and Rice 70
Refreshing Watermelon Sorbet 96
Rhubarb Pie 89
Roasted Brussels Sprouts 54
Roasted Brussels Sprouts, Chicken,
    and Potatoes 73
Roasted Mushroom Risotto 61
Roasted Turnips 45

S

Salmon and Edamame Cakes 58
Savory Yogurt Bowls 38
Scallions Omelet 30
Sesame Breadsticks 67
Simple Pear Crumble 47
Simple Pork and Capers 75

Simple Veal Chops 65
Smoked Salmon Egg Scramble with Chives and Dill 31
Southwest Tofu Scramble 35
Spanish rice 48
Spiced Fruity Cookies 53
Spicy Baked Sweet Potatoes 101
Spicy Cabbage Dish 74
Spicy Chili Salmon with Lemon 67
Spicy Enchilada Bake 99
Spicy Tomato Shrimp 101
Spinach and Beef Meatballs 73
Spinach and Endives Salad 51
Steel-Cut Oatmeal with Plums and Pear 33
Strawberry Yogurt Smoothie 127
Stuffed Breakfast Peppers 37
Stuffed Sweet Potatoes 42
Sweet Potatoes and Apples 44
Sweet Potatoes with Coconut Flakes 34
Sweet & Sour Pork Chops 115
Sweet Yogurt with Figs 34
Sweet Zucchini Pie 84

T

Tasty Roasted Broccoli 103
Tasty Tortilla Bake 113
Tofu & Green Bean Stir Fry 58
Tuna Sandwich 111
Turkey Wrap 114
Turmeric Endives 41
Tuscan White Beans with Shrimp, Spinach, and Feta 114

V

Vanilla Apple Mix 94
Veggie Sushi 76
Very-Berry Mug Cake 50

W

Walnuts and Asparagus Delight 109
White Bean Stew 103
Whole Grain Pancakes 28
Whole Wheat Baking Powder Biscuits 26

Z

Zesty Yogurt Pots 51
Zucchini Beef Sauté with Coriander Greens 119
Zucchini Pad Thai 69
Zucchini Tomato Bake 56

Printed in Great Britain
by Amazon